MYSTICS AND 1

"Because I get several request a day to blurb or review a book, I have to refuse most of them to survive. But I opened this fine book out of curiosity, and found it so well written, and so filled with gems, that I knew I had to pass on the good news! Read *Mystics and Misfits* by Christiana N. Peterson—even if you think you don't have time."

—**RICHARD ROHR**, OFM, founder of the Center for Action and Contemplation

"I cried healing tears as I read *Mystics and Misfits*. Christiana N. Peterson's breathtaking way with words, coupled with her rare perception, left me pared back and longing for the deeper, more honest things of faith. Anyone grappling for words to express the strange intertwining of joy and suffering needs to look no further."

—**AMBER HAINES**, author of *Wild in the Hollow*

"Christiana N. Peterson is a bridge-builder: her great gift is the ability to connect the mundane world of the here and now to saints and mystics and ways of seeing and believing that seem distant, strange, and forbidding."

—**GREGORY WOLFE**, editor of *Image*

"*Mystics and Misfits* is a generous invitation to join the saints in everyday conversation about the marrow of life and essence of faith. If you are looking for spiritual companions for your journey, Christiana N. Peterson is ready to offer worthy introductions to Saint Francis and others. With candor and care, Peterson creates a new conversation for those who are hungry for deeper goodness."

—**KELLEY NIKONDEHA**, author of *Adopted*

"*Mystics and Misfits* is achingly beautiful. It is like a long love letter to holiness. The mystics with whom Christiana N. Peterson engages are ones who wanted so much to be holy, as Jesus asked us all to be, and did it in ordinary and extraordinary ways."

—**JON M. SWEENEY**, author of *Francis of Assisi in His Own Words*, from foreword

"In Christiana N. Peterson's beautifully told memoir, the reader comes to understand that our relationships with saints living and dead can take many forms but that, at their heart, they are about the compassion that draws us into community."
—**KAYA OAKES**, author of Radical Reinvention

"*Mystics and Misfits* is part memoir, part biography, part handbook, and entirely wonderful. *Mystics and Misfits* is a practical and intelligent introduction to the spiritual wisdom of figures as diverse as Francis of Assisi, Margery Kempe, and Dorothy Day, yet it is also a personal story, at once gentle and deeply inspiring."
—**CHRISTIE PURIFOY**, author of Roots and Sky

"*Mystics and Misfits* is an imaginative and spiritually rich look at the reality of following God in community with a great cloud of witnesses past and present. In the tradition of Kathleen Norris and Madeleine L'Engle, Christiana N. Peterson finds the wildness of God's mercy at work in her ordinary life. Rich and resonant, this book speaks to all who dare to hope that the God of Saint Francis still speaks to us today."
—**AMY PETERSON**, author of Dangerous Territory

"*Mystics and Misfits* is the perfect blend of idealism tinged with mortality, of contemplation marred by depression and the mundane realities of moldy rugs. This is a gorgeous, quirky, and heartfelt book inviting the reader to love the mystics and misfits of our world—both those around us currently and those who came as guides long before."
—**D. L. MAYFIELD**, author of Assimilate or Go Home

"This unflinching narrative of spiritual transformation will first captivate and then challenge readers at the depths of their souls. Despite their eccentricities, the mystics model a deeply human, resilient faith that offers sustenance and hope as Peterson navigates a perilous journey from youthful idealism, through disillusionment, and to a more authentic life."
—**MARLENE KROPF**, professor emerita of spiritual formation and worship at Anabaptist Mennonite Biblical Seminary

MYSTICS

AND

MISFITS

Meeting God through St. Francis and Other Unlikely Saints

Christiana N. Peterson

HERALD
P R E S S

Harrisonburg, Virginia

Herald Press
PO Box 866, Harrisonburg, Virginia 22803
www.HeraldPress.com

Library of Congress Cataloging-in-Publication Data
Names: Peterson, Christiana N., author.
Title: Mystics and misfits : meeting God through St. Francis and other
    unlikely saints / Christiana N. Peterson.
Description: Harrisonburg : Herald Press, 2018. | Includes bibliographical
    references.
Identifiers: LCCN 2017048471| ISBN 9781513801643 (pbk. : alk. paper) |
    ISBN 9781513801650 (hardcover : alk. paper)
Subjects: LCSH: Mysticism. | Spirituality--Christianity. | Mystics. |
    Christian saints.
Classification: LCC BV5082.3 .P48 2018 | DDC 248.2/2--dc23 LC record
    available at https://lccn.loc.gov/2017048471

To my Grandmama Oneta,
the first mystic I ever knew,
who loved reading novels
about a medieval Benedictine monk who solved mysteries.
Thank you for making it okay to stay up too late reading.
And
to my daddy, a bit of a misfit.

Contents

Foreword

I SUSPECT THE CHURCHES of my childhood were even less open to saints and mystics than Christiana N. Peterson's were. We were nondenominational Baptists in Wheaton, Illinois, and saints were regarded as not just beyond the pale; they were wrapped in papist superstition, designed to lead faithful believers away from Christ.

Ironically, just as Peterson found her adult denominational home among Mennonites, it was also among Mennonites that I was first favorably introduced to saints. At age seventeen, having found no support at church or home for registering as a conscientious objector to military service, I contacted the Lombard Mennonite Peace Center for help. There, Mennonites taught me the peace and justice traditions of the church, and handed me *The Nonviolent Alternative* by Thomas Merton, for which I'm eternally grateful. They, that book, Merton, and the many threads of connection to follow changed my life.

That was nearly thirty-five years ago now, and the churches of my childhood have also changed—or, at least, are changing. I find an openness to the message, historical figures, and spiritual practices pondered in Peterson's thoughtful book, *Mystics and Misfits*, even among communities that were once highly suspicious of anything that smacked of Catholicism.

As Peterson makes clear, the saints are not the property of Catholics anyway. Saint Francis and Saint Clare (two of my favorites) and thousands of others are there for everyone, Catholic or not, even Christian or not. We can't conceive of the vast mystery of the kingdom of God.

This book is achingly beautiful. It is like a long love letter to holiness. The mystics with whom Peterson engages are ones who wanted so much to be holy, as Jesus asked us all to be, and did it in ordinary and extraordinary ways. So you'll encounter phrases here such as "lunacy of love" and "miracle of attention"—not because people like the thirteenth-century Francis of Assisi and the twentieth-century Simone Weil accessed God in ways that elude the rest of us, but because they were countercultural, as one surely must be to live like saints.

Hence the title: *Mystics and Misfits*. Anyone who has met Jesus or knows the gospel also knows that living up to the gospel is to somehow be, essentially and vitally, apart from the world around us. The saints seem to have figured this out, and yet they still, most profoundly, enter back into that world in order to transform it.

Most enjoyable for me are the occasions in this book when Peterson reveals how one of these complex, devout followers of Christ discovered, often from the church's edge, a unity with God that led others to look to her or him for some guidance. Peterson explains the personal appeal of looking to mystics in her prologue: "[Their] unequivocal experiences of God began to challenge the heady intellectual faith of my childhood."

I know that feeling. These days I turn to the saints daily to try to stay the course that those blessed Mennonites put me on long ago.

—Jon M. Sweeney,
author of *Francis of Assisi in His Own Words*,
The St. Francis Holy Fool Prayer Book,
and many other books

Author's Note

THIS BOOK is not meant to be an exhaustive overview of the Christian mystics. Instead, my intent here is to dialogue with the mystics who have been companions with me and to introduce some of my readers to the mystics for the first time.

There is an overwhelming amount of reading and research material on each of the mystics, particularly Saint Francis, who is likely the most popular saint and mystic who ever lived. But because Saint Francis wrote so little about his ministry, there is much conjecture and difference of opinion about his life. I was heavily influenced by Julien Green's *God's Fool* and Jon Sweeney's *The Enthusiast*. Sweeney's book made Francis more accessible to this non-Catholic, and it also worked well for the purposes of this book, which aims to show the complexities of a life lived in Christian community.

While the specific stories of the life of Saint Francis came from outside sources, I took some artistic and literary license in my retelling of his story and Clare's story. In this, I consulted Julia Walsh and Joan Weisenbeck, both members of the Franciscan Sisters of Perpetual Adoration. Having said that, any mistakes in those retellings are purely my own.

I discovered the works of Howard Thurman, an African American mystic writing in the twentieth century, in the later stages of my writing process. I hope to discover and learn from more mystics of color, and I hope that their voices will be magnified in this renewed interest in the Christian mystics.

Some of the events I describe in this book can be seen from varying perspectives. If anyone who has lived at Plow Creek disagrees with my telling of events, I apologize for any offense caused by what I've written. I have tried to be honest about the challenges we've encountered, about these moments that were significant to me, to our family, and to our community, and about my own failings. These words came from my own limited perspective and from my own understanding of the stories I was told by members of Plow Creek. Some of the names of individuals in this book have been changed.

I hope that my experiences, hurts, and mistakes can help others practice love and lean into community life with more openness. Any mistakes are mine and mine alone. Ultimately, I hope that the people I write about—both living and dead—are honored. Thank you for reading.

—*Christiana N. Peterson*

Prologue:
Mystics

*M*Y LOVE of the mystics started with a garden statue of Saint Francis of Assisi.

I almost missed it when we were cleaning out my grand-mother's house, taking what we could, hoping some of it was useful and could be passed down to our children. My grandmother, in her nineties and suffering from dementia, had just been moved to an assisted living apartment.

I walked by the patio doors and glanced out the glass pane and saw the wooden back of Saint Francis. The statue was a gift from my dad to his mother. I'm not sure she knew much about the saint. Even if she had, Saint Francis, with his care of the poor and love of animals, would be a safe saint, even for a traditional Protestant like my grandmother.

The statue of the saint and mystic is carved out of one log, and the arms and small details could be scraps from another. It's a nondescript figure, one that neglects the details of his face, his bald pate, the folds of his garments, in favor of the simplicity for which Saint Francis himself lived and died: more stick figure than illustration, more idea than image.

When I saw him, cobwebs were draped between the birds on his outstretched arms, dust was lodged so deep in the wood grain that it would never scrub off, a strand of rope was tied at his waist, and his eyes (two simple slashes in the wood) were closed in peace; I loved him.

Growing up in the Church of Christ, a low-church tradition that endeavors to follow the ways of the first-century church as the apostle Paul wrote about in his letters, I was taught that we were all saints. The word for "saint" used in the Bible, in both Greek and Hebrew, essentially means the same thing: someone who is holy, godly, set apart. By this definition, none of us are saints except by God's grace and love. Paul writes in the first few verses of 1 Corinthians that all are spoken for, all are loved, and all are called to live in the love of Christ. So by God's grace, all are called to be saints. How, then, could we venerate certain people who are considered to be saints, set apart and considered holier than the rest of us?

When my husband and I decided to send our eldest daughter to kindergarten at a Catholic school, I'll admit that I had some concerns. Having migrated through various denominations before settling in with the Mennonites, I was excited that she would have a Christ-centered education. But I couldn't help thinking about the warnings from family and friends who were steeped in Protestant traditions and skeptical of Catholic school indoctrination (which certainly included lessons about those dreaded saints).

I think my daughter learned early on *not* to tell me when she prayed to Mary or to her guardian angel at school. I could see the beginnings of a grimace as her innocent prayers led to my excruciating theological explanations about why we don't need a mediator to pray to Jesus for us (except for the Holy Spirit). But the indoctrination came more gently than I expected, and it came not to my daughter but to me—in the form of homework coloring pages about Saint Therese, Saint Francis, and Saint Patrick. It turns out I was the one being educated.

I stumbled upon the beautifully broken statue of Saint Francis around the same time that those kindergarten coloring pages quietly introduced me to the lives of the saints. Though I knew less about Saint Francis than many of my peers did, as I read about Saint Francis and other unlikely saints, I noticed something interesting. These men and women, the ones I thought were "holier than thou," would never actually call themselves "holy." In fact, they often harped on their own fallenness.

As I was drawn to Saint Francis and other saints in so many areas of my life, I began to relate to them not as saints but as mystics: complex, devout human beings who lived on the edges, who longed for unity with God. I began to see them as people who didn't always fit: literally, misfits. Maybe they had some things to teach me.

* * *

The word *mystic* makes many Christians imagine New Age practices, gift shops full of crystals and Wiccan paraphernalia. But this is not the whole story: although mysticism is a part of most religions, it isn't another word for pagan rituals. The word *mystical* (which in Greek means "hidden") has been a part of the Christian church since the second century. Christians of these early centuries used the word *mystical* to describe a unity with God that was more profound than "the literal sense of the scriptural texts and stories." Mystical theology was a branch of study that focused on ways of knowing God not with the mind but with the deepest part of the soul.[1] Often this included contemplative practices and prayers. Mysticism meant leaning into a deeper relationship with God, and that relationship encompassed more than just knowledge, intellectual assent, and rational belief.[2] In the early Christian church, mysticism wasn't something apart from the church or other theological ways of thinking, but instead was understood in light of its relationship with the church's doctrine.[3] The oldest recorded Christian mystics were a part of the church.

Although it is difficult to characterize all mystics, it's safe to say that mystics have vivid experiences of God, search to know God beyond logic and doctrine, and find their lives transformed because of these encounters.[4]

Saint Francis and other Christian mystics captured me in a time of desperation. I was struggling through mental health issues and outside stresses, and I had reached the limits of an intellectual faith. I saw that in their own times of suffering, the mystics had encounters that led to unalterable transformation. I longed to be changed by God, too.

Many mystics experienced visions, moments of rapture, altered states of consciousness, and sometimes extreme bodily transformations like Saint Francis's stigmata, in which the marks that Jesus received at his crucifixion were found on the saint's hands, feet, and side.

I used to dismiss such intense encounters as fabricated, a product of mental illness, or just a wishful interpretation of an odd state of consciousness or unconsciousness. In fact, some medical scholars believe that the wounds Francis received and eventually died of were actually caused by leprosy, that the disease could even explain his stigmata wounds.[5] It's not surprising that scientists might try to rationalize a miracle like the stigmata. Our brains and bodies can do wondrous and terrifying things. For instance, I often see things in my room in the middle of the night: a childlike gnome who might be nefarious, a faceless monster, a slightly deranged rabbit. After a few moments, I can usually shake it off and convince myself I was dreaming or in some state of hypnagogia, the transitional state between sleep and waking during which some people experience hallucinations or sleep paralysis. Sometimes I wonder if I'm seeing something real, something my mind wouldn't allow in the daytime.

Maybe the mystics were seeing things in this same state of unconsciousness. Maybe Saint Francis's stigmata were really just a horrible disease. Maybe it really was all in their heads. Or maybe, just maybe, the mystics experienced truly miraculous things and had visions that were the result of years of contemplative, prayerful preparation to encounter God.

But visionary encounters with God aren't easy. The mystics will point us to strange journeys and winding paths. After all, the mystics could be odd. If we imagine meeting some of these pillars of the church today, we might diagnose them rather than venerate them. With their seemingly strange behavior and visions, we might lock them away in psych wards instead of hailing them as heroes of the faith. The mystics often seemed to live on the edges of the church, society, and even mental health. They were not only mystics but *misfits*: people who were often ill-suited to their time, culture, and church, and who were conspicuously different in their way of being in the world.

What was it about them that set them apart? Were they intentionally trying to be different, or was it God's transforming power in their lives that simply made them less interested in social climbing, in power, or in prestige for their own sake? Randy Harris, author of *Living Jesus*, said that the mystics are less apt to be seduced by worldly things than theologians and preachers are.[6]

"When you give yourself to the life of prayer," Harris said, "it's by nature a case of constantly admitting your powerlessness."[7] That's not to say that the mystics weren't interested in being influential or prophetic. Mystics like Saint Catherine of Siena and Saint Bernard of Clairvaux bent the ear of popes and kings. Howard Thurman, an African American mystic-prophet, wrote in the 1950s about Jesus' message of hope for the marginalized. Many of these mystics longed to sway the tide of injustice toward the God who lived with the suffering.

Mystics like Dorothy Day, Margery Kempe, Clare of Assisi, and Simone Weil—whose lives and ideas began to sustain me and my family during some challenging times— were dipping into a powerful spiritual stream. This stream led to the river of life, but it also carried them, at times, into darker tributaries.

As I read their letters and biographies, the mystics' transformative, unequivocal experiences of God began to challenge the heady intellectual faith of my childhood. With his philosophical musings on thoughts and knowledge, the apostle Paul was beloved in my childhood church tradition; after all, he told us in Philippians 3 that he wanted to "know Christ." In my spiritual immaturity, I thought that what he spoke of was a knowledge of the head. I believed that if I could just be certain about all theological things, then my faith would be perfect.

But I missed the rest of the passage. Paul continues, "I want to know Christ—yes, to know the power of his resurrection and participation in his sufferings, becoming like him in his death, and so, somehow, attaining to the resurrection from the dead" (Philippians 3:10-11). Like the mystics, Paul wanted to participate in a relationship with Christ. The word in Philippians is *koinonian*, or fellowship. It's a word associated with community, with mutual belonging, with a relational participation. Paul wanted more than an intellectual knowledge of God; he wanted to actually be crucified with Christ, to be in community with the suffering God. I think the apostle Paul was a mystic too.

***

It was my own experience with *koinonian,* or community, that led me to the mystics. Living in a Mennonite intentional community on a farm in the rural Midwest has led my husband, Matthew, and me to some beautiful experiences. But it has also been fraught with challenges. My faith grew out of times I spent in spiritual wilderness.

Most of us came to intentional community because our general culture was ill-fitting for us. For years after we moved to the Midwest, I didn't see myself as ill-suited to "normal" culture. But I think the years have turned me into someone a little closer to a misfit.

Some people have referred to our lifestyle in our small community as "the simple life" or "living simply." Our life in the past eight years has been delightfully unique. These years have been full of the blessing of children, friendship, and fellowship. Yet we've also experienced sorrow and suffering that we never would have imagined when we first moved there. It's been weird and it's been painful and it's been suffused with joy—but it hasn't been comfortable, and it has been far from simple.

When I found Saint Francis, I recognized that his way of living was far more radical than our modern notions of "the simple life" would suggest about him. I began to see his sideways wisdom, the dirty details, and the ugly beauty of his "simple" message.

* * *

In his own way, Saint Francis points me to a life that is radical and challenging. From the outside, his way looks idealistic: love of nature, simplicity, and kindness. But when I draw nearer to the way of Francis and, ultimately, the way of Jesus, I am confronted with my own inability to move and change, like a physical force that turns me back in on myself. In his book *The Gravity of Sin*, my friend and fellow writer Matt Jenson talks about sin being like a man curving in on himself. I want to be transformed, but I can't jump ahead on the journey with the force of my own will.

The statue of Saint Francis, a little bit broken, stands in a spot by my porch among the pots of rosemary, pink fairy vines, and fallen leaves. My messy corner of earth is not worthy of him. But I don't think he would mind. He reaches out with wooden hands that have no divided fingers. He welcomes us. He welcomes our guests. He calls to the flesh-and-blood birds, which will surely defecate on him.

Even though I am a bit wary of his openness, I still keep him there at my front door. I suspect that walking along-side Saint Francis will push me closer to the Christ whom he saw in a vision, a vision that left him with the stigmata wounds that would fester until his death. I am afraid, though, and I fight against my tendency to turn inward. I am afraid because I suspect that any encounter I have will probably leave me scarred for life, too.

Letter to Saint Francis:
The Skirt of God

Dear Saint Francis,

I imagined I saw you today out of the upstairs window. Your cowl had slipped off your head, and you were fighting uselessly with the wind to put it back up again. The recently fallen leaves around your feet likely understood the inevitability of your struggle.

Your habit, patched and torn and patched again, was the same dull grey as the maple tree under which you stood. I almost missed you, but your stigmata were bright red flares that caught my eye. I wanted to ask you so many things, but I decided not to come, to stay inside, and I can't take it back. So here is a letter for you, tucked into the hollow of our maple tree, in case you return and I'm not here. I'll leave it just above the place that you were standing, where a few red leaves cling to the flaking tree bark like the wounds on your hands.

Seeing you out there on such a day, when fall is about to concede defeat to winter and the wind howls like the coyotes in our woods, reminds me of a longing I've been feeling. Longing seems to be an active, unarticulated sort of restlessness. Maybe melancholy is the gloominess of a long-term, unfulfilled longing.

When I was a twentysomething and in grad school in Scotland, I took a road trip to the northeast tip of the country with my flatmate, Jen. We met our painter friend Genevieve at a castle near Wick, right on the North Sea. Genevieve's oil paintings were hanging all over the cottage where we stayed: haunting, otherworldly pictures of rooms with trees growing out of the middle of them. It was as if her canvases were precise renderings of the feelings this place had evoked in me from the moment I stepped into it. I'm not sure if I felt melancholy then or if it was just a youthful longing. Perhaps both. Maybe the woefulness of my younger years in Scotland was like a town on the volatile North Sea: bleak and lovely, home to some eccentrics and hearty folk, haunted by the terror of the people it drove to madness.

Sometimes this feeling seemed like the wind at Genevieve's little castle, a persistent, unending tone somewhere between a wheezing and a whistle. A patch of yellow daffodils between the castle and the sea only made the place feel sadder, like the effect of bright flowers in a cemetery, emphasizing the contrast of life and death more painfully.

I'm not sure why I speak to you of this longing, Francis. Maybe it's because I've been suffering recently from these swirling, anxious thoughts. So, in desperation, I began practicing centering prayer, and that led me to mystics like you.

How did you know what to do, Francis? Was it when you heard the voice of God the first time that you decided it was time to let go of the things that bound you? They're about your encounter with Christ, I think, those mystical experiences. Can you show me how to be a mystic? Because contemplative prayer is troubling to me. I don't think it is working.

I've always thought that the experience of God should feel mystical. That it should take me out of my ordinary and into fantasy—that God should speak out of light, thunder, a dramatic stage or song. Or maybe an angel could show me how beautiful wings really are: dreams of fairy sightings made real.

That's what I want from my "God experience": a fulfillment of this longing for something strange, for something intangible, fantastical, mystical, this longing for something beautiful. Isn't that how the ancient mystics encountered God? My experience of God seems to take a different form.

When I practice these prayers, I try to focus on being in the presence of God. But the darkness swirls behind my eyelids into psychedelic shapes of animals and concentric circles. When my alarm goes off to free me, I don't feel mystical at all. Only sad.

Is this what is meant to happen when I sit in God's presence? Am I meant to feel more uneasy, more confused, and more sad? Am I meant to cry and wish for something a little more lovely? I mean, why can't I be like the mystic Teresa of Ávila and see my soul as a castle? Do you think it could be a fairy castle?

Now that I'm thinking of it, the longing I described in those paintings and in the visits to the North Sea—somehow it feels like the longing of a young girl. One who is just discovering that her old belief system isn't quite her own yet. One who longs to jump into a beautiful painting or be a part of a great romance or fairy tale.

I'm older now, and I still haven't outrun the longing. It's here in my heart, but now it's not a niggling discomfort—one that leads me into the melancholy of a night by the North Sea. This aching slashes at me now. I sometimes feel it like a clawing inside, scratching to get out and find purchase. Sometimes it feels as though it will burst through my skin and show itself on my flesh.

Do you understand, Francis? I watched you outside; you held your arms out to our maple tree, like the first tree hugger, before "tree hugger" became a derogatory term thrown at left-wing hippies. And you did something curious. After you hugged the tree, you put your fingers in the holes where my husband taps the tree each year for syrup and then you wiped your hands on the bark. It was a childlike gesture, one that reminded me of the way a child wipes his hands down his mother's skirt after a meal. He can't wait to remove the foreign substance as much as he can't wait to feel the tender strength of his mother, the one who keeps him alive, the one he treats the best and worst.

When I went outside, you were gone, of course. But I still approached the place you'd been. I touched the spot on the grass. There was a disturbance there, but it was slight enough to be imagined.

But there, there on the tree where your hands had run up and down the grey bark, were two red streaks, dark, almost black as blood.

Did it hurt or heal to feel the bark scratch those deep rankling wounds? Or was it that longing you felt, aching to get out, that tore you inside until it broke through your skin? Is that why you rubbed your hands against the tree, because it makes you feel close to the skirt of God?

It seems that you and I have switched places, Francis: I am longing for joy and you are stuck in sorrow. Though I suspect you have a glimpse of what it means to live with both.

I want to know so much, Francis. Please, come back, another time. I think I'll make a better choice on your next visit. I'll come out to greet you and ask for a dance.

Your friend and failing mystic,

Christiana

PART I

SIMPLICITY

Pure holy simplicity confounds all the "wisdom of this age" and the wisdom of the flesh.

—Saint Francis of Assisi,
"Praises of the Christian Virtues"

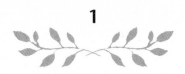

1

The Vague Adventurers

*A*N OLD WHITE BARN sat alone, looking ill at ease on the flat canvas of a farm field. The muddy road ahead of us led straight into the trees. Unused irrigation links were thrown in a pile, and we were blocked in by the woods on three sides.

We had just turned at the sign for Plow Creek Farm. We knew we were so close to the community we'd been seeking. But we weren't there yet.

We were lost.

* * *

My husband and I decided to move to a commune on a whim.

A commune sounded like the adventure Matthew and I longed to have together, our first as a married couple. We'd only been married a year and a half and had a six-month-old daughter. Our courtship and marriage had been certain in love and spontaneous in its speed. And almost exactly a year after our wedding, we were holding our baby girl in our arms.

But that whirlwind of spontaneity had finally gotten us stuck. We were tire-deep in the mud of a farm field in the middle of the Midwest. Our car tires groaned and spun with each punch of the accelerator, splattering mud like black buckshot. Matthew eased his foot off the pedal.

It was technically spring. In fact, it was April 1, the very day we'd met two years before. Those two years ago, I had just finished four years of grad school in Scotland and was nearly thirty, with no career ambitions except as a writer and with a deep longing to meet someone. I was living in Texas and had the job of trying to get college baseball players interested enough in World Literature to pass their class so they could play their sport. Not exactly a vocational dream.

I spent some afternoons at my friend Jessica's house imagining my future husband, wondering if he actually existed, if I'd always be single. Jessica had developed a nickname for my future spouse: "Sweater," so named not for his habit of perspiration but because she was sure he'd be a geeky professor type who wore glasses and sweaters with patches on the elbows.

A few months into my time back in Texas, Jessica sat me down and said her sister had found the guy for me. We'd gone to the same university in Texas but we'd never met because he was two years younger than I was. The only bits of information she could offer were these: in his college years, he had ridden around campus on his bike (in Texas, an unusual habit for college students, who are usually addicted to gas-guzzling pickup trucks); he had a mop of curly hair; he had an affinity for poetry; and he spoke German in his sleep.

It was not much to go on, but we already had a connection in the sleep department. My family loves to tell the story of the time when I was in elementary school and I managed to make it down the stairs in the middle of the night. My dad found me sitting in front of a blank television screen with the remote in my hand.

When we were first introduced over email, Matthew and I were separately descending from our own adventures—he from the Peace Corps in West Africa, and I from graduate school in Scotland. I hesitate to admit how I had chosen Scotland over another grad school location. It reveals the romantic, emotive, and self-absorbed way I have made some major decisions in my life. That I even had a choice is a desperate sign of my privilege. But here it is: I decided to move while listening to a song by Enya on *The Lord of the Rings* soundtrack. The song, with its Celtic musical influence and some of its lyrics sung in the Elvish language created by Tolkien, transported me to the mysteries and magic of the bleak highlands. As I listened to the music, I was that girl who wished Middle Earth were real.

Matthew's Peace Corps adventure had begun not with a song but with an intriguing poster hanging in the hallway outside one of his classes during his senior year of college. I don't know what the poster looked like, but I picture it like the one that hangs in his office now: an action shot of four barefooted boys jumping off a cliff into a murky body of water. The caption reads: "Life is calling. How far will you go?"

Matthew and I emailed, then talked on the phone, then met for the first time on April 1 those two years ago. It only took a few days for us to begin talking of love and marriage. We were engaged after only a few weekend visits to each other's towns, and six months after our first meeting, we were married. We connected immediately because of shared wanderlust, an expanded view of the world, and even a reevaluation of our childhood church tradition.

I moved to Washington, D.C., where he was already living and working at a nonprofit for international development. D.C. seems to be a holding place for many a former Peace Corps volunteer, and my husband was no exception.

As it does for many young people who move to D.C. with dreams of social justice, the sheen had soon worn off for Matthew, who spent his days in a cubicle doing paperwork and his breaks playing cribbage with other unsatisfied young do-gooders.

It wasn't long before Matthew and I both began to struggle with questions about life and vocation. Although his job was technically doing good things in the world, he was never able to see the tangible differences he made in anyone's life. After spending his days pushing paper, he found the most satisfaction outside of work, doing various hobbies and especially tending our plot at a community garden a mile from our house in D.C. I had recently quit my job at a local florist and was discouraged in my search for a publisher for the young adult novels that no one wanted. Even though I'd found a group of mothers to be a part of, most of them were employed, and I was lonely in a new city.

So I wasn't too surprised when Matthew came home one night after walking our puppy, Jasper, marched up to our bedroom where I was nursing our daughter, Neva, and declared, "I think we should move to a commune."

I don't know what response he expected from me. All I said was, "Okay, as long as it's Christian."

I'd heard of intentional communities and communes from my grad school flatmate, Jen, who'd lived with several other young people during a stint in the Lutheran Volunteer Corps. She'd told me of a rural Lutheran community in the mountains where they farmed and shared common work. Romantic that I was, hippies and misfits were idealized figures in my mind. For Matthew, his desire for a unique way of doing community was influenced by his time in a small village in West Africa, the farming he'd done with a local man in that community, and perhaps the caption on that Peace Corps poster. Life was calling us. Adventure was only a few thousand miles away.

When we began searching online for a commune, we were surprised to find a whole database full of them. It was rather easy to decide which communes were not on our list. These included the "adult-only" communes, in which participants were encouraged to share sexual partners, as well as those communes that were awaiting the end of civilization or the apocalypse on a specified date.

And then there was an unassuming and fairly modest little entry about Plow Creek, a simple Mennonite-affiliated community in the rural Midwest. The chaos of their website—with its ugly background the shade of an avocado that has been left in the fridge too long—might have deterred some, but in my unfettered eagerness for an adventure, I chose to see it as charming. It was clear from the pictures of folks at the community that simplicity, both in dress and in the 1980s quality of the photographs, was at least an unspoken value.

And simplicity, among other things, was what Matthew and I longed for, even though we weren't quite sure what that meant. For us, simple living was certainly about healthy, local food; we were discovering writers like Michael Pollan, Wendell Berry, and Barbara Kingsolver, who were all passionate about the need for local food and local communities. But it was about something else too. Something vague and noble, adventurous and beautiful.

In those weeks before our visit, we corresponded by email with a member of the community named Louise. I contributed questions typical of someone whose only knowledge of Mennonites was from a Christian novel I'd read in high school. As a teenager, I'd absorbed very little about their theology and a lot about how they dressed and lived: in plain clothes like the Amish, with no electricity. I wondered, Who *are* the Mennonites? I knew they were respectable, but what did they believe? And did I have to wear skirts and cover my head to live there?

Louise assured me that, even though some women chose to cover their heads, Plow Creek community members were not Old Order Mennonites or Amish Mennonites in the way of my childhood novels. There were no dress codes, and although the Internet was shoddy, it worked. I would learn later that the members of the community came from a diverse mix of backgrounds and that, even though the community members were affiliated through church membership in the regional Mennonite conference, they were not typical Mennonite (if there even is such a thing).

After a string of conversations with Louise, we tucked our daughter into her car seat and drove from D.C. to Illinois, stopping in Kentucky to search out the home of Matthew's favorite author, Wendell Berry, the spokesperson of idealistic, farm-loving dreamers everywhere.

As we edged closer to the Plow Creek community for the first time, I noticed that the farmland was flat and the miles stretched out on either side of the highway in a forlorn and unhidden way. Hailing from generations of Texans and having gone to college in Abilene, I knew about flatlands. I'd heard of West Texas pioneer wives going insane from the uninterrupted whistling of the wind. But I spent most of my life amid the cedar trees of the Texas Hill Country, where highways dipped and curved across the county, cutting through ancient walls of limestone. I had a fondness for trees and hills. We hadn't even arrived and I was having doubts that I could mentally withstand the bleakness of the landscape.

But a few miles from the community, the road began to descend as it followed the terrain into a valley. The community was a mile from a small village, population seven hundred, that was prettily situated in a valley of trees and hills dotted with large, old houses with wide front porches and high gabled windows. It was a no-stoplight town, with a railroad running across the edge of Main Street and two small, well-kept parks bracketing the town.

We passed through the village and saw a green sign for the community pointing out of town. We found ourselves driving parallel to the railroad tracks, and half a mile later, that weary white barn at the front of a field with a sign that said "Plow Creek Farm" came into view.

* * *

When I thought of moving to a Christian "commune," I liked the countercultural images it conjured in my mind: hippies who hugged trees, who tilled the earth in homemade clothes, and who loved their neighbors. But the truth is, we knew very little about what we were getting ourselves into.

Plow Creek began when a few young families arrived at the community property in the 1970s, buying the 180 acres with—I'm told—$10,000 in cash. They lived in the dilapidated farmhouse on the property and in nearby rental houses until they could build up the community—both the infrastructure and the physical buildings—with their own labor. But the word *commune*, which I'd pictured dreamily from our house in D.C., was a loaded term in the minds of many of the older folks at Plow Creek. It reminded them too much of the free-love communities of the 1960s and '70s, communities for which the founders of Plow Creek were trying to offer a Christian alternative during the "back-to-the-land" movement.

So not long after we arrived, I was told in no uncertain terms that Plow Creek was *not* a commune. It was an intentional community. *Intentional community* is an umbrella term that can refer to anything from housing co-ops to communal farms to ashrams to communes. Many intentional communities are not Christian. "Intentional" is perhaps a misnomer anyway. Many communities and churches are very *intentional* about certain aspects of their life and worship. But what generally defines an intentional community is a focus on building relationships, sharing both the physical and emotional burdens of land or housing, coming together around shared values, and often having an egalitarian style of decision-making. Although we didn't know the precise details at the time we visited, these qualities, along with a Christian vision, described Plow Creek as well.

As we drove toward the community, we supposed that if we decided to live there for very long, we might eventually be asked to share finances with others. We weren't sure what that looked like, and indeed, those requirements had changed over the years of Plow Creek's existence. The earliest members in the 1970s had shared almost everything, from income and savings to cars and houses. They had stipends for the smaller necessities of life, but for the larger expenses, they spent meetings discussing what was appropriate to spend money on. That became too overreaching for many who arrived later in the life of the community, and the members decided to trust one another more with expenses. Eventually, few people were willing to share finances or give up their savings and assets. Levels of membership in the community's bylaws and rule of life were changed in the later decades of the community in order to reflect that.

* * *

After a few moments of our tires spinning in the mud, Matthew freed the car, reversed all the way back to the white barn in the Plow Creek Farm field, and consulted our directions. A few wrong turns later, we reached the top of a hill and nearly missed the faded hand-carved community sign. Taking the sharp right-hand curve, we drove down the gravel road, passing several winters' worth of stacked firewood, and rounded a corner. There was the meadow; six simple buildings dotted the circular drive.

Our adventure—of a different sort than we expected— was about to begin.

2

Interlude:
The Simple Saint

*F*ROM *GARDEN CENTERS* and big-box stores, to eBay and even gas stations, figurines of Saint Francis are everywhere. Most of these collectibles are meant to emphasize Francis's softness and saintliness. It's humorous, really. What would Francis, the man of radical poverty who slept on the ground and ate with lepers, make of his idealized likenesses placed next to our trinkets, our shelves of books, our embellished picture frames, our insignificant stuff and more stuff?

I hope he wouldn't mind my garden statue of him. The wooden figure I pilfered from my grandmother's house is cracked at the elbow. It stood outside on an uneven garden patch beside the front porch, but a windstorm knocked it over. The morning after the storm, as I ushered my children out the door for school, my daughter cried, "Oh no! Saint Francis has fallen!"

I got the children in the car, and even though we were running late, I dashed back to the door to pick him up and set him aright. Something deeper than sentimentality made me cry out when I saw that his wooden arm was split. Inside, a rod connected his forearm to his elbow. I tried to shove it back together, but there was no time.

So I carried him inside and placed him beside the couch. Now, instead of facing our maple tree, he faces my bookshelves, the disarray of living room toys, and his small porcelain likeness. Every time one of my children passes by to get to their toys, his arm falls off again.

My children have learned how to reattach his limb and the birds who won't stay notched to his footstand or good arm. I find his foot on the table behind the couch sometimes.

I like to think Francis would appreciate and encourage the crumbling of his statue.

* * *

Not long after I brought Saint Francis's garden statue to our house, the deadline for my daughter's Catholic school religion project for kindergarten approached. Since one of the options was to write a report about a saint, my daughter and I both chose him as our patron (of sorts). Francis is not only our patron but the patron saint of animals, ecology, environmentalists, and even the Humane Society. If there were a Christian Hippie Association of Farmers (we might call it CHAF, for short), I imagine Francis would be the patron saint of that too.

The miracles and life of Saint Francis, who was born in twelfth-century Italy, have filled the pages of books ever since his lifetime. Francis's simple approach to life and the gospel, his grace, and his joy attract numerous followers. And he makes a habit of baffling his companions.

On one occasion, he leaves his followers on the road and runs toward a flock of doves and crows. Instead of scattering into the air—as birds are wont to do when they are startled—they wait for him. He begins to preach to these birds, who, in turn, seem to actually listen to him. He tells them that they are noble and clothed and protected by God. In response, his feathered congregants "stretch their necks, extend their wings, open their mouths, and gaze at him." Before he leaves them, Francis blesses the birds and sends them on their way.[1] They fly in four companies—one to the north, one to the south, one to the east, and one to the west—spreading out in the directions of the sign of the cross that Francis had made over them.[2]

Another time Francis asks a boy, who is taking turtle-doves to market, if he will let Francis set them free. Moved by the odd fool's gentleness, the boy gives up his birds to Francis, who gently chides the birds for allowing themselves to be captured. He frees them, and they roost and lay eggs near the home of his friars.[3]

Perhaps there is no story more legendary than that of Francis and the wolf. Francis hears word of a wolf that has been harassing the people of a town named Gubbio. The animal has prowled the countryside, eating resident's animals and, on occasion, the townspeople who try to defend themselves. Francis's heart goes out to the people of Gubbio, and he determines to help them. With the whole town watching, Francis gently approaches the growling wild animal. Just as the wolf springs at him, jaws open for attack, Francis makes the sign of the cross. The wolf drops down at the saint's feet, chastened. In speaking to the meek animal and calling him "Brother Wolf," Francis learns what the wolf needs: he is hungry. Knowing that all the wolf requires for a reconciled relationship is to be fed, Francis negotiates a peace between the wolf and the people of Gubbio, a peace that holds until the wolf's death years later.

Francis's love and care for creatures extends even to inanimate objects: to rocks and flowers, to trees and sky.

There are stories of Francis saving worms and bees, collecting lost paper in case the words of Holy Scripture are written on them, and walking tenderly over rocks. He even composes his famous song, "Canticle of the Creatures," naming the moon, the sun, the wind, and the water as his brothers and sisters.

Francis especially shows radical love for the poor, the sick, and the marginalized. Once, while on the road before his conversion, Francis meets a knight returning from the Crusades. The knight is poor and his clothes are ragged. Francis, dressed in wealthy clothes bought by his father, is moved. He removes his own expensive cloak and gives it to the knight.[4]

Eventually, Francis will become like the poor knight, dressing only in the most humble of clothes. He will give away all his possessions, rejecting his father's wealth. He will live like a beggar, and he will become a saint.

3

First Impressions

*A*SIAN BEETLES collected by the hundreds on the windowsill of Louise's guest room. I watched them bouncing back and forth across the ceiling during the night, like the chomping fiends in an old video game, and wondered how many more could fit in the room. Where would they go when the windowsill and ceiling got too crowded? Would they begin dropping onto my baby, sleeping peacefully in a Pack 'n Play at the foot of the bed?

That day we had finished a few visits with Plow Creek community members and had gone to church on Sunday in the upstairs of the common building: a simple red building with a wooden cross nailed beside the door. It wasn't much to look at. The floor was a faded linoleum, spotted with old designs and yellowed by years. There was no decor to speak of, except hooks for homemade church banners that would be arranged for worship. But the view out the windows made up for the lack of decoration. Behind the building, the woods were wild and expansive. In front of the building were the willow tree and well-mowed meadow that had hosted years of children's games, wedding ceremonies, dances, and concerts.

As we lay in bed watching the bugs trail each other, Matthew and I compared observations. I didn't recognize half the people in the community from the photos on the website. Many of the pictures were so outdated that some of the people at the community weren't even pictured. Like a couple about our age who both had striking red hair.

I noticed the couple sitting at one of the long white tables in the common building. I noticed Matt and Angela because, well, they looked more like us. Many of the other men had long scruffy beards or Amish-cut beards with no mustache. Even though it wasn't at all required, several of the women wore scarves or head coverings, long hair, and long skirts. A few of the members, with bare feet and a scruffier approach to grooming, leaned hippie instead of conservative.

I don't suppose I could have articulated then why I felt more comfortable with Matt and Angela, but they seemed more like *us*. They were around our age; Matt was a visual artist and Angela was a doula and an herbalist and worked for a consulting firm from home. They just felt easy to be with, more like our friends and church family in Washington, D.C.

We had been attending a Lutheran church in D.C. that had warmly welcomed us into its struggling flock. It had been around for a very long time, and some of its elderly members—one of whom had gone on a date with John F. Kennedy when she was a young woman—remembered being in the youth group there. A third of the members of the congregation were white and elderly, a third were from several countries in Africa, and a third were African American. They gave us a baby shower when Neva was born and were so excited about the first new baby at the church in ten years.

But something was missing for both Matthew and me. It's a problem inherent in a certain part of D.C. culture. Of course, a large portion of the city's population had been there for generations and wasn't a part of the city's over-educated, success-driven inhabitants. But I wonder if many of the churches in downtown D.C. were so accustomed to the transience of a portion of their congregants (young pro-fessionals like us) that attendees found it better to keep to themselves outside of church life. Or maybe it runs more deeply in our culture as a whole. I think it's a characteris-tic of many American churches: members love seeing each other during worship each Sunday, but when it comes to knowing each other and sharing lives outside the building, many are more hesitant. Perhaps the effort to truly share our lives with others is a messier business than we want.

So in D.C. I was a lonely new mother trying to make close friends with moms who worked full-time and with the lovely people at our Lutheran church, who seemed to be mostly satisfied with seeing each other just once a week. But in that common building at Plow Creek, it was clear that folks not only knew each other well but were involved in one another's lives throughout the week. They cared for each other, worked together, and worshiped together. I didn't know yet the challenges we would face, but I knew there was something there that we'd been longing for, some deeper connection and intimacy.

The houses and buildings on the property had been built by the community members themselves when the commu-nity was started in the 1970s. Like the red common build-ing, the structures were simple but sturdily constructed, with functionality taking precedence over aesthetics. We were in Mennonite land, after all.

Because there are so many ways of expressing Mennonite values, it's not always clear where this simplicity fits in. Mennonites certainly have a history of simplicity in dress, in the materials they used, and even in their way of approaching communication and theology. And many have lived out their simplicity through nonconformity to the world, by focusing on living out the poverty of Jesus, by living in rural or farming communities, and even in their adherence to holiness.[1]

We noticed the diversity of the group too—a strange and wonderful hodgepodge that was unique for a small midwestern town. There were people and families of all ages from countries like Indonesia, Haiti, Guatemala, and Estonia as well as the United States.

Most of our observations only added to our interest in and excitement about becoming a part of this community. But when it came to discussing the actual people we met, we realized that our reception was mixed. We felt welcomed, but we also felt from certain folks a measure of cautiousness. Those we met had chosen to live outside of mainstream society. For some, this had a lot to do with discomforts and social anxieties. For others, it was an intentional choice to reject cultural and societal norms.

Another reason for their caution was something we would later experience ourselves. Having never lived in intentional community quite like this before, we didn't yet know about visitor fatigue.

When Saint Francis first began attracting followers, many people—folks who had known him as a child and were confused or angered at his sudden message of simplicity—thought he was a community hopper, one who stayed in one monastery after another. In one of his books about Saint Francis, author Jon Sweeney uses the term *gyrovague*, which refers to a type of monk who was actually condemned in the Rule of Saint Benedict: "These spend their whole lives tramping from province to province, staying as guests in different monasteries for three or four days at a time. Always on the move, with no stability, they indulge their own wills and succumb to the allurements of gluttony."[2]

I wonder if folks at Plow Creek were reticent because they wondered whether we might be a few more gyrovagues: community-hoppers discontented with status quo life but content to wander and take advantage of the hospitality of others. Hosting visitors, especially gyrovagues, can be exhausting and even at times painful for communities like Plow Creek, as Matthew and I would later discover.

Many types of people are attracted to intentional community. Some, like Saint Francis's gyrovagues, float from community to community. Some like to come for a time to learn and help out before moving on to other things. Others are longing for a family they never had. A very small percentage of these people are serious about joining the community.

When we visited, I doubt that anyone was quite sure what type of guests we were. Even though we were treated to meals and generous hospitality, we were only three of many who had received such kindness over the course of months and years.

With very little deep thought, we became the type who moved there.

During our April visit, Matthew met with the two farm managers. We were pleasantly surprised that they offered him a job on the spot. He'd be in charge of strawberry operations. In order for Matthew to start work on the farm on June 1—two months after we visited—we quickly packed up a Penske moving van and made the arduous road trip from D.C. to Plow Creek.

The Plow Creek buildings and land were owned by the people who shared finances. Since we weren't ready to become financially communal yet, we began by renting one of three apartments in the Valley House on the property, where we shared a laundry room and a large backyard with two other families. The valley housed several barns, the cow and pig pasture, and a half-acre community garden. We had access to the meadow, the common building, and the other houses by a trail that led up a steep hill.

That first day at the community, I stood by the moving van and held Neva as our new neighbors and farm interns gathered around to help us move into our apartment in the Valley House, giving us their generous offerings of cookies, fresh strawberries, and moving muscle. A maple tree stretched toward our front porch, offering shade on that late spring day. The Valley garden was our front yard; the barns, tractors, and woods surrounded us with a combination of wildness and order that felt right in the midst of the nervous excitement of our adventure. Everything seemed beautifully simple.

But simplicity was still a word that we didn't really understand. As Saint Francis said, true simplicity "confounds all the 'wisdom of this age' and the wisdom of the flesh."[3] It would take a lot more time for us to understand that this kind of wisdom is hard won.

4

The Simple Life

TWO WEEKS after we moved to Plow Creek, I was surprised to find a teepee being erected in my backyard. A family with seven children who were members of the community was busily constructing the life-sized shelter with wooden pikes that reached up past the height of our roof. Eventually I learned that my house neighbor—redheaded Angela, who lived with her husband, Matt, in one of the three apartments in our house—had a friend who wanted to give birth in that teepee.

The matriarch of the community family who owned the teepee was a midwife who would deliver the baby. Angela, a doula, would also aid in the birth.

In my idealistic excitement, I wasn't even frustrated that no one had asked if it was okay with us that someone was going to give birth in our backyard. I figured this was a part of our new lifestyle: that sometimes people gave birth in nontraditional places (or, if I thought about it another way, in way *more* traditional places than we tend to give birth in now).

I'm not sure that even Angela had expected the full-sized teepee to be erected just fifty feet from the double sliding-glass doors that looked out onto the backyard we shared. She thought the mother would eventually break down and deliver the baby inside their house.

A thunderstorm was forecast that evening, and we thought it might interrupt the birth plans. But the mother would not be deterred. Matthew and I woke in the middle of the night to thunderclaps outside our open bedroom windows. In the darkness, I could just see the outline of the teepee. Then, when the lightning lit the backyard as if it were daylight, the teepee came alive, full of smoke, fire, and the rain from the fateful thunderstorm. The thrumming of the rain seemed to rise and fall with the mother's cries with each contraction.

When I woke to the early light of morning, I stood at the window and heard the newborn's very first cries. And despite the strangeness of it all, I cried too.

The weirdness and beauty we'd been longing for was being birthed right in our backyard. Perhaps the romantic notions I'd had in D.C. were not so unrealistic.

In fact, my other notions of our life here were already becoming a reality: the trickling streams and the calm rocking of the wind through the trees when Neva and I sat on a blanket in the afternoon, the cloud shapes barely visible through the firmament of extended branches and leaves that shaded us. I daydreamed of an older Neva running through the fields and picking blueberries at random. We wanted her to know the life that humans have known for centuries, a life close to dirt and potent smells in which she'd know which season a zucchini squash grows in, and what an ear of corn tastes like fresh from the stalk. We wanted her to get muddy and snowed on, to be hot in summer and cold in winter, to feed chickens and pick so many strawberries that her fingers were red with the juice.

We wanted to be able to call her to dinner from the woods and the creek.

I guess Matthew and I had each been craving the same things: deep relationships and something out of the ordinary, some place to live out simplicity, to grow and to serve and to teach Neva what was important in life.

Most of all, we wanted her to know God, to live in a community that helped her be a faithful member of creation, to love and know her neighbors, and to be known and loved by them. I suppose we wanted her to have the life of Saint Francis—bucolic and good. And maybe she'd even end up a little bit like the mystic. Perhaps this birth was just the beginning of an extraordinary life with our wonderfully quirky and authentic neighbors.

In the weeks that followed the teepee birth, Matthew was thrown into the deep end of his first farm season. The farm's major moneymakers were berries, particularly strawberries and blueberries. The farm team was composed of three families, as well as seasonal interns. Meanwhile, a woman named Adrienne managed the Valley garden, a large, half-acre space that provided food for market, food for community shares, and lastly, produce for Creekers (the nickname for those who lived at Plow Creek).

Matthew was often out the door before I was awake. He came home in the evenings exhausted from the physical labor of weeding acres of strawberries, walking the fields to get a sense of their readiness, standing in the sun for hours while customers came and picked their own berries, and managing pickers in the early mornings before markets opened or farm orders came in. When farmers' market season began, he would be gone until ten some evenings. Having come from a nine-to-five D.C. job, he (and I) found this to be a big adjustment.

Matthew soon began to learn the names of the different types of strawberries—Jewel, Darselect, Earliglow,

Honeoye—so that he could recommend them to customers who would come to pick them themselves in high season. He returned from his first few days sunburned and hungry. I quickly had to learn how to balance cooking bigger portions with not eating too much myself; after all, I was not outside walking the fields all day like my farmer husband, working up an appetite. I began to cook nearly every meal, and since we didn't have a dishwasher, every day I was left with mounds of dishes to do. When harvesting began in late July and August, several women taught me how to preserve tomatoes, salsa, and applesauce. Others shared with me their lists of summer and fall preserving, which included hundreds of jars of canned vegetables and fruits and quarts of blanched and frozen food. Learning to use the local food we grew was a busy pleasure.

I was occupied with the new duties of a farmer's spouse as well as with trying to learn new skills like making yogurt, weeding, feeding chickens, and keeping my doors unlocked for neighbors who dropped by throughout the day. Most of the time, I actually liked it. It felt like the opposite of the loneliness of living in D.C.: fullness, or the correct amount of busyness. Although we were off the beaten path, we were not solitary or isolated.

* * *

Adrienne was the one who showed me, goofy city girl that I was, how to feed chickens. She was five months pregnant and wearing a bonnet, and I followed her under two electric fences, through the horse stables, and around barbed wire (which I scraped myself on and she did not) to her chicken coop. She shushed the birds into the coop with her skirts, and I was wistfully reminded of Laura Ingalls Wilder.

Eventually, Adrienne asked if I wanted to share chickens with her. That way, we could share chores and duties and also get the benefit of eggs. But in order to do that, we would need to buy more chickens.

From Adrienne I began to learn that living "the simple life" often means spending a large percentage of the day performing the time-consuming but rewarding tasks of daily living: growing and cooking your own food, tending to the garden and animals, mending and sewing. But Adrienne didn't live simply because of some notion that it was hip or cool. This way of life was under her nails, in her worn skirts, in the steam coming from a summer kitchen dedicated to gardening and preserving food. Having grown up on a farm, she knew how to save a penny, stretch a meal, patch a garment, and, in this case, get laying hens at a discount.

"If we want more chickens," Adrienne told me one day, "we'll have to catch them."

"Catching them" would mean driving twenty minutes to another farm that was selling their year-old laying hens. When we drove up to the farm, Adrienne groaned at the sight of the small temporary coop in which the chickens were being kept. She was expecting to have more room to catch them. The coop was about waist high, and four feet by seven feet.

Because Adrienne was pregnant, I realized as we approached the coop that it was going to be up to me to "catch them." Knowing that I would have no idea how to go about this task, Adrienne called out to me: "Grab them by their feet and turn them upside down. It makes the blood rush to their heads and they go limp."

So I crouched down into a squatting position—the only way I could get to the chickens without bumping my head on the roof of the coop—and lunged. Chickens are surprisingly fast, and my first attempt caused mass chaos. As they scattered, their wings flapped and slapped at my face. But chickens are also not that smart, and before long I learned how to grab them. If you can get one foot or even a good hold on a few feathers, then you've caught one.

I eventually got my rhythm, grabbing chicken after chicken and handing them off to Adrienne. She tied their feet together and put them three at a time into large paper bags.

After about a half hour's work (which included chasing a rooster who had twisted out of his rope), we were finished and on our way back home, the two roosters and twenty-four hens tucked into their bags in the back of the truck. Adrienne had watched another expert farmer bag roosters in the same manner, so she'd been confident everything would be fine.

We were energized when we pulled up to Plow Creek. I took Neva from the neighbor who'd been watching her, strapped her onto my back, and helped Adrienne unload the bags of chickens into a wheelbarrow to take them back to our coop.

But something was wrong. Some of the chickens weren't moving. We rushed the wheelbarrow back to the coop and released the chickens bag by bag. At the bottom of each bag, crushed and suffocated by its friends, was one or two dead chickens, eyeballs white and feathers sweaty and still warm. The poor things had pooped themselves in fear.

Saint Francis wouldn't have been impressed. But we wouldn't have blamed him. We felt terrible.

After that, we had to decide what to do with the dead chickens. Six of them we'd planned to give to friends, who were going to butcher them anyway. But three were now *our* dead chickens and we had to take care of them before rigor mortis set in.

After dinner, Adrienne came to our backyard in the dark, and we hung the chickens on a tree limb. She taught me how to skin them and cut off their heads. Then we went inside and disemboweled them on our kitchen cabinet. I felt oddly removed from the whole thing and was only truly bothered by the blood spurting out of the severed neck and the first touch of the intestines inside. Some parts of the experience were even fascinating, like the soft-shelled eggs forming inside their bellies that, after washing, would be ready to eat.

Later that night, in our fridge and freezer sat two free-range, fresh and local chickens. That week I cooked them up and served them proudly to my family. As I cut into the chicken for my first bite, I was partly heartsick that they'd died inhumanely. But I also felt empowered by the fact that I had provided good food for my family, from start to finish, with my own hands.

Chewing that first bite, however, I realized that the chicken was dry and tough. Perhaps she was punishing me from the great fowl beyond.

* * *

A year after moving to the farm, we were busy with the "simple life" as it would look in a less pristine version of an issue of *Country Living*: a life that included a house that seemed to blend in with nature itself. Dirt and straw from Matthew's boots left trails in the mudroom and up the stairs, mold collected on the walls from a humid summer with no air conditioning, and bugs got in. I found myself obsessively vacuuming those bouncing Asian beetles from the corners of my sliding glass door after they flew in through holes in the screens on the open windows, bugs released by the harvesting of the acres and acres of soybeans from our neighboring farmers every fall. In the glow of sunset, you could see them, billions of them darting like particles in a ray of light.

The beloved Saint Francis—at least the pristine version of legend and picture book, preaching to the birds and saving a town from a wolf—might have been proud of our lives (besides our chicken killings, of course). These early obsessions and minor annoyances became, if not welcome, at least tolerated signposts of farm life that marked the seasons' passing. Like those rays of light that showed the flying insects, our life was dreamlike in its beauty. Even after a year, life in community was still a delight.

5

Interlude:
The Spoiled Charmer

S AINT FRANCIS'S STORY can be easily distilled down
to some very attractive points: his care for all the
earth's creatures, his love for the poor, his radical simplicity, his passion for peace instead of war, and his joy. All
of these things are the reason that Saint Francis means so
much to so many. His life is a dream for hippies, liberals,
activists, back-to-the-landers, ecologists, intentional community folks, and young evangelicals interested in caring
for God's creation.

I mean, who wouldn't want to walk with this saint on a
path to Jesus?

Although he had many early biographers, it was
Franciscan Brother Ugolino whose stories of Saint Francis
in his book *The Little Flowers of Saint Francis*—so innocent
and open in their vision of faith in a loving God—became
some of the most popular legends about the saint. The

stories tell us as much about Francis's followers as about the actual man himself. Even if they are embellished, as many scholars suggest, these stories are lasting. There was just something about Saint Francis, and about the experiences of those who knew him, that makes these stories believable. As Franciscan scholar Jon Sweeney says, "Fantastic things *did* happen, and although the stories about those actualities were often inflated, they had truth about them."[1]

But those who know Francis only for these lovelier portraits—a free-spirited hippie who took a vow of poverty, a gentle man who preached to the birds and called the sun his brother and the moon his sister—might be surprised to learn another side to him. Just as there's more to simplicity than I knew at the beginning of our life in community, there's more to the story of Saint Francis than we care to acknowledge.

The popular legends are wonderful, but the other Saint Francis seems infinitely more interesting: the man who gained followers without trying, who loved with a strange and simple love. The darker stories of his life are infused with the mystery and imaginative beauty of truth. As it turns out, Saint Francis as a young man was spoiled, unchecked, selfish, and arrogant.

* * *

Francis is born to a wealthy family in Assisi, Italy, around 1181. He enters the world just as Europe is moving out of the so-called Dark Ages and into the Middle Ages. The feudal system is weakening, a middle class is emerging, and the wealthy people (like Francis's father) are getting wealthier.

When Francis is born, his father, Pietro di Bernardone, a merchant who has built up his own wealth, is away on business. Francis's mother, Pica, is not alone, though. Even as this baby's weight drags at her insides till she feels she'll be emptied out and hollow, she is somewhat relieved that her husband is away. She is in the company of women, women who move with ease as they hold their hands to suffering, to blood, to the transparent membranes that tremble between life and death. When Francis breaks through to life and breath, dark-headed and small, his olive skin sparkling through the redness of the afterbirth, Pica sees a vision of Elizabeth, the mother of John the Baptist.

Maybe Pica senses that her son will one day be venerated. Or maybe she is drawn to the story of the cousin of Mary from the Bible for reasons that we cannot know. Regardless, before her husband can return, she christens her baby Giovanni, after John the Baptist—the man who, like Francis, gathered followers and was called a holy fool because of his penchant for dressing in rags.

When Pietro returns home from the business trip, he is furious at his son's Christian name. In a sense, what motivates Pietro is probably what still motivates those of us caught up in the American dream. His focus is on building wealth and passing it down to his children. This is a relatively new concept in the twelfth century, when the middle class is growing stronger. Pietro isn't religious, and because he has built up his own wealth, he doesn't appreciate Pica's religious vision of his son, named after a strange hairy dude who lived poor and wild. Maybe Pica pleads with him, or maybe she is a woman resigned to her place: she already knows she has no voice. Pietro renames the boy to his liking. Because of his father's love for France—the place Pietro had been doing business when the baby was born—Giovanni becomes Francesco, or Francis for short.

Francis isn't a handsome child, but his exuberance and his love of song attract lots of little followers, even as a boy. He spends his days singing the French songs his mother learned as a child in Provence and living up to his father's name for him. Maybe he is an imaginative child, playing with knights, slaying dragons, or racing sprites. He loves the bees and butterflies, and captures insects only to set them free and admonish them for being captured in the first place. His playground is the pastoral setting of Assisi, where his father's wealth offers comfort and ease.[2]

Eventually, Francis grows into a young man who is indulged and pampered by his father, a silk merchant who dresses his son in the finest clothes in order to show off his wealth. Francis attracts other rabble-rousing youth who are glad to help him spend his father's money on booze and parties. During his teens and early twenties, Francis becomes a wild partier who can easily gather his friends for a good time; they are known as "the Merrymakers." Some accounts of his exploits with the Merrymakers suggest they engage in vandalism, theft, and other kinds of debauchery.[3]

Although Francis and his friends spend a lot of time in idleness and mindless pleasure, he is also known for his generosity, his joyfulness, and his charm. Even before his conversion, he takes up the practice of giving alms to the poor. On one occasion, while he is working in his father's shop, a beggar enters. Francis is helping his customers, wealthy aristocrats and their tailors who travel from neighboring cities to buy cloth from Pietro di Bernardone. The beggar—his filthy, tattered clothes even more muted next to the multicolored bolts of cloth on tables throughout the store—approaches Francis with cupped hands, calling, "Alms, alms!" Even the usually unruffled merchant's son is appalled.

Francis glances at his customers, who have turned away in disgust. "Go! Get out of here!" he shouts at the poor man, shooing him away as he had never done before, even to the bees of his childhood.

The beggar leaves the store, and Francis returns to his customers. They applaud his efficiency and ruthlessness, laughing about the "dirty beggars," the "eyesores" who occupy their streets.

A winged shame flits and taps Francis's shoulders, finally landing heavily in his consciousness. Francis drops a bolt of cloth midsentence and runs outside. The beggar hasn't gone far. Indeed, he almost seems to be waiting for the young Assisian.

"Please, please," begs Francis, grabbing the poor man's hands. They are moist with the pus of open sores, rough with the crusts of scabs and disease. Francis, overcome with revulsion, pulls away and reaches into his pockets.

"Please, take this. Please, just take this." Francis drops the contents of his pockets in the man's open hands. The whisper of wings, of shame, still sounds in his ears.

The beggar bows and then raises his arms to the sky. He whispers, "You will be venerated one day, young Francis." Then he shouts, "You will be dressed in these rags and dance before popes!"

Francis backs away, turning to run, the shame tingling down his neck and spine. When he gets back to the shop, he turns back to look for the beggar.

But the beggar has vanished. In his place hangs the outline of a pair of wings.

6

The Smell of Simplicity

OUR FAMILIES were decidedly weirded out by our strange choice to move to an intentional community. It's not that they were surprised or even unsupportive. After all, they were used to both of our somewhat spontaneous adventures as single people. But Matthew and I were married now, and had a child. "How will this work?" they probably wondered. "And what kind of people are they linking themselves to in this community?"

Some friends and acquaintances, when we visited them, would respond to our life on the farm with, "Oh, how I envy your simple life." Maybe our rural setting seemed far from the rapidly moving concerns and worries of their city lives. Or maybe farm life seemed idyllic, close to nature with singing birds and frolicking animals and sweet-scented plants.

They were partly right, and our initial view of simplicity actually wasn't far from theirs. But this kind of simplicity was mostly concerned with our physical lives. In that sense,

Plow Creek Farm seemed, at first, to tick off all the boxes of simplicity: we didn't have traffic, there were few places to shop, and access to entertainment was limited. We were closer to the earth and the seasons, and it was calming to hear the wind, the creek, and the chugging of a tractor instead of the police and fire engine sirens of our neighborhood in D.C. We ate food from the farm, and we lived off the land, which was a lot closer to the way our ancestors lived for millennia than the way we'd been living in D.C.

In some ways, we idealized our new adventure the same way some people idolize Saint Francis as a funny little hippie who preached to the birds. Both views focus on the sweetness and the beauty, but without any knowledge of what is actually a strenuous way of life.

The idea of living simply appealed to Matthew and me for many reasons. We had both grown up in wealthy homes, but our upbringing and travels—largely possible because of that wealth and privilege—had exposed us to people of different cultures and economic backgrounds. Just after the Soviet Union fell in the 1990s, my father took my older sister and me to Russia. We visited a poorly funded children's hospital and sat in the homes of many widowed women who fed us—even as they recalled recent memories of standing for hours in breadlines and of the family members they'd lost to the secret police. We'd visited these places briefly, though, and then I would return home, glad to be back to my normal comforts, satisfied with myself and what I'd learned from their stories.

But my father was pulled back to Russia time and again. I think he wished that Russia, and not our American culture of ease, were his normal life. In his younger years, my father was frequently troubled by the ethical and theological responsibilities of having money. It seemed that this reticence with money spurred him to share what he had: During his overseas travels, he helped to begin the first radio program to share the gospel after the Soviet Union fell. He encouraged his church to write letters to prisoners who heard the gospel for the first time. He helped start a theological college in Saint Petersburg. He paid for the ongoing education of people in Ghana, Russia, and the United States.

I don't know if he continued to agonize over money as he grew older; he didn't share that with us, his family. What I do know is that all the time he spent with others also came at a cost. When he traveled, my sisters and I often felt bereft of his presence and affection. Like many men of his generation, he was gone a lot, he didn't communicate well, and he wasn't emotionally available.

From a very early age I was confused by the tension I felt: I loved the comfort our life provided but I also was torn by guilt and shame for being so privileged. And it took becoming an adult and moving to intentional community to understand why. My guilt about wealth was really about the complexities of economic injustice and what wealth can keep us from.

If you're wealthy, you aren't as acquainted with inconvenience. New cars don't break down as readily. You live without fear of what an expensive illness could mean. The rising prices of food or gas don't register on your worry radar, healthy teeth aren't a luxury, and your children can participate in every after-school activity they desire.

In moving to Plow Creek, Matthew and I were being led by the discomfort we felt with our privilege. We wanted to allow ourselves to be a little less comfortable, to be in community with those who understood what it meant to struggle, and to maybe place ourselves within that struggle a tiny bit more too.

But the truth was, that tension remained, and sometimes I longed for what I left behind.

Our simple house at Plow Creek seemed to amusingly resist my cleaning efforts. Surfaces and floors were swept and mopped and vacuumed, but it was only a few hours before the house settled back into its old routine of rural decor. The toilet and showerhead continued to look unclean thanks to the grime from iron in the well water. Cobwebs hung all over our house—between a picture frame and a lampshade, the showerhead and the ceiling.

The humidity of summer introduced the smell of moldy rugs, and I thought about newer houses in cities with air conditioning and updated carpeting. Where the crown moulding was decorative and not merely functional and the paint was fresh and aesthetically pleasing. When I was on my hands and knees scrubbing the inside of the toilet bowl with baking soda and steel wool, I thought of clear city water and refrigerators with ice machines. I imagined a larger kitchen and more than one bathroom. While I shooed away the fruit flies that hovered around the small compost bucket under our sink, I fantasized about garbage disposals, tightly sealed houses, and nice restaurants that would do the cooking and dishes for me.

I didn't always have those feelings. But sometimes when a family member came for a visit and wondered aloud how I was able to live like this, I began to see the dirt in the caulking as if it were a neon sign. Before I went back to Texas or on a trip to any big city, I often felt unprepared and that I never had the right clothes to wear. My unease was akin to those nightmares of being naked in public, and I was certain people were looking at my secondhand clothing and feeling sorry for me. I should wear makeup, I'd think—the makeup that sits in the drawer that my daughter, playing dress-up, opens more than I do. I should actually brush my hair.

But I found that no one cared much what I looked like at Plow Creek. Clothing was functional. What else would it be for? Why would anyone put on mascara when she would be spending the day in a hot kitchen, sweating from canning? Who would wear a new white lacy blouse on a day of gardening and weeding? Sensible shoes were necessary for hard farm work. Accessories on hot days were superfluous.

When Matthew and I drove all the way from Plow Creek to Texas during our first January on the farm, I noticed for the first time how dramatic the culture clash was between where we were living and the place I grew up. Until we came upon big-box store after big-box store on the outskirts of the Dallas suburbs, I hadn't thought about the intense culture of shopping and consuming in which I had grown up. And I was a little ashamed of the way I felt when we drove by outlet malls and shopping centers. I sighed audibly, feeling the warm effervescence of pleasure that comes from the sights and smells of consumerism.

Living at Plow Creek didn't take away my desire to dress well. I got that feeling when I went into a clothing store just before Christmas and the fleece snowflake pajamas were on sale and the smell of artificial pine trees was in the air. I still wanted to buy sweet-smelling candles, music and books from the chain bookstore, the pretty scarf that I didn't need, the overpriced shirt I'd only wear once.

I don't think it's wrong to go shopping, or to want to look nice, or to dress up, or even to find artistic satisfaction in fashion. But people at Plow Creek didn't care if I was dressed well. They just wanted me to show up at church and common meals. They wanted me to care about the members of the community. They wanted support and friendship and prayers.

Sharing a washer and dryer with two other families, well water that stained my showerhead, hot water that often ran cold from overuse in the winter, living in a house that would never feel spotless and always smelled a little funky, wearing my thrift-store sweater, trying to budget our food for the month: somehow, through it all, I felt a profound sense of joy and contentment with our version of the simple life.

7

Interlude:
The Colors of Poverty

*L*IKE MANY YOUNG MEN of his age, Francis had his imagination captured by legends of knights and dragons. The images bleed into reality, however, as he watches the bold nobility dressed in armor, riding through the town in their cavalcades, caught up in skirmishes with the nearby Perugia. Francis decides to join the war effort.

But his romantic notions are crushed by the blood and bones of his peers who are slaughtered in battle. The enemy only spares the nobles whose families are rich enough to pay a ransom for their battle-thirsty sons. Being one of the rich few, Francis spends some miserable months in a war prison, caring for those of his compatriots who grow ill around him. Eventually he becomes ill himself.

He entertains his fellow prisoners with his mother's French songs and the story of the beggar who came to his shop and called him a saint. The memory of his shame with the beggar comes darting back to his shoulders. And he hears the words of the beggar's whisper: "You will be venerated one day, young Francis."

Maybe I will be a saint, he chuckles to himself.

But the shame whispers: You think you can be a saint? In his dreams, he sees a cross, his winged shame nailed to it. When he wakes, he's confused to find the world is grayer, less full of the bolts of color that filled his childhood, more muted like the beggar's rags.

Francis returns home, ill and ill at ease. As he lies in bed those weeks and months, he imagines something to brighten the bleakness. He thinks of Saint George and the dragon, a tale brought back from the Crusades of the heroic soldier who rescued a grand lady, a princess, from a dragon. The story once again washes Francis's world with the colors of heroism: red for the flag of the Crusades, silver for the armor of a knight, green for the dragon whose blood is spilled. As he recovers some of his strength, the bleak colors grow bolder and brighter.

The colors of poverty are briefly forgotten in favor of the vitality of battle. Francis decides to head back out to battle with one of his prison companions. This time it's to slaughter the Muslim infidels in the Holy Crusades. On this ride to battle, he passes another beggar hunched over in shabby clothes. The memory of the vanished beggar from the shop returns to Francis. He stops his horse and dismounts. As he approaches the beggar on the road, he realizes that this is not a poor man but a knight who has lost all nobility and has been reduced to poverty.

Francis's heart is moved. He sweeps his expensive cloak off his shoulders and wraps it around the poor knight. Colors mute and flicker. Francis gets back on his horse, feeling afraid, fearing that the colors of his joy and life will continue to mute. But he shakes his head, focusing on the red-and-white Crusade flag. The colors brighten again, and he and his companions continue on their holy Crusade.

Days later, however, illness interrupts his knightly pursuit. In his sickness, Francis dreams of a Lady, as noble and beautiful as the princess Saint George rescues from the dragon. In his vision she urges him to return home.

Does this Lady really need to be rescued from a dragon? Or is she someone else: a Lady who will be the one to save Francis from himself?

When Francis returns home at the Lady's wishes, the colors don't return. Even in his father's shop, the vibrancy of the bolts of cloth is subdued in the grip of this melancholy. He stops spending time with his friends, and they begin to gossip behind his back. When some of them are finally able to rally him into some more merrymaking, he wanders away during a party.

When his companions finally find him, Francis is murmuring absurdities. They laugh at him. Something has happened to the childish merrymaker.

Francis is lost.

8

Decay

ONE SPRING EVENING a large fire started on the hill near the meadow. All I could see from our house in the valley were the clouds of smoke pulsing and billowing over the trees. Matthew ran up the hill while Neva and I watched the half dozen or more fire trucks and ambulances sweep by our road to race up the hill. We waited anxiously for news.

The news was not good. One of the newer homes on the Plow Creek property had burned down. In the end, it was a blackened and gutted outline of the beautiful house that once was.

The large family, whose mother had midwifed the baby in the teepee in our backyard, was living in the house at the time. We were thankful that, besides some minor burns, no one was physically injured. But most of their possessions were destroyed, and the smudges of ash and dirt couldn't hide the shock and sorrow in their faces.

The house had been lovingly crafted in the 1990s by the people of the community. The firefighters, who put out the fire and therefore saved the rest of the buildings on the hill, told a newspaper reporter that the house was so well built and well insulated that it was difficult to fight the fire.

But not long before the fire, some unresolved conflicts had flared up between the family who lost their home and other community members. The community's decision to swiftly remove the crumbling and charred remains of the burnt house, because of safety concerns, added more pain to these emotional wounds. Now, displaced by the fire and with broken relationships and feelings already raw, this family wanted more time to search through the ashes for their belongings. Accusations were made, and motivations were questioned on both sides, until the family left the community for good.

The fire was revealing some pain and losses among the group that I didn't really understand at the time. Memories from the community's past were being stirred, opening wounds that had never healed and exacerbating the division and brokenness that started well before the flames began.

Our eagerness for adventure, to make a difference, and to live a life of simplicity initially shielded us from the harsher realities of what life was truly like in community. We were tired in the exhaustion of farm life, yes, but our youthful, wide-eyed wonder kept us plowing through work stress and community quirks.

But gradually we began to discover that the community had been dealing with both decades-old trauma and more recent discord. This fire had many implications for the community, and soon after the fire, we began to understand some things about the past.

Not long after we moved to Plow Creek, we began to hear the name Conrad, always mentioned in tones that hinted at pain and loss. It took us a while to realize that the whole community was still living under the shadow of Conrad, and that his actions would cause turmoil for years to come.

Almost two decades before our arrival, Plow Creek had been a vibrant community. They owned several houses in town, they had their children in the local schools, and they ran a doctor's office as well as a construction business. From what we were told, the community was very ordered and had high expectations of its members. Gardens were kept neat, and every adult had responsibilities: cooking community meals, running programs to keep the children involved in community work, building houses, preserving food. The worship was lively, annual holidays were celebrated, and members shared finances, approaching work and play as one. Though some found this exhausting, the order helped the community function and run. There were mistakes and failures, but it seemed to be a thriving community.

But then Conrad—a founder of Plow Creek, one of its most trusted elders, and the regional Mennonite conference minister at the time—confessed to the members at Plow Creek that he had sexually abused a minor. The details of Conrad's betrayals were hazy for those of us who weren't around in the 1990s. But we would learn many years later that Conrad had abused other underage victims as well, and that he hadn't disclosed this during the process in the 1990s.[1]

I can only imagine the trauma experienced by those whom Conrad abused. I have wondered many times throughout the years who they were, and how they managed to piece life together after this violation. Many members of Plow Creek were themselves survivors of sexual violence, and the fact that Conrad had committed these abuses brought back their own traumas. While nothing comes close to the trauma experienced by those whom Conrad abused, many members of Plow Creek were left with a deep sense of broken trust and violation because of Conrad's actions.

Over the next decade, Plow Creek lost over half its members. The few who chose to stay after what became known as the "Conrad mess" in the 1990s were those who still managed to hope that God could repair the deep sense of brokenness. But there was so much damage to overcome. I understand that Conrad had been a charismatic, authoritarian leader, one who was a strong proponent of emotional intimacy, deep personal sharing, and group decision-making. After Conrad's secrets came to light, members were understandably less trusting of the careful structures they had built to care for one another. And they were especially suspicious of leaders. They relaxed some of the expectations and demands of each other. Over time, since they needed more folks to move to the property, they relaxed their expectations of them too. For a formerly strict community, the ethos began to look a little more like "live and let live."

That's how we all came to be there: the older folks who had given many years to community, the family with seven kids and even more pets, the war resisters, the families who turned out to be more interested in a bucolic place to raise their children than community, and the younger folks who wanted to share life but were not interested in sharing finances.

No wonder we were struggling in the fire's aftermath. The community was embroiled in years-old conflicts, living with the legacy of a leader's abuse, unable to affirm new leaders, and yet still trying to work and live out a vision.

* * *

In the middle of his second farm season, mere months after the fire, Matthew suddenly found himself in charge of the farm. The farm manager had been overcome by addictions and had left in the middle of the season to seek treatment. Matthew, with only one season of farm experience under his belt, was thrown into the stress of managing a farm. As Matthew began to learn the business from his position of leadership, he was realizing still more difficult things about the farm. All of it began tearing at the fiber of our dream of the simple life. Because of the lack of strong leadership on the farm, the berry plants hadn't been managed well or cared for, the soil was depleted, and morale was very low.

At the same time, the community began to have meetings with the intention of establishing a new vision. But the meetings seemed to circle round and round, beginning with one purpose and extending into another for months on end.

In my naïve optimism at the time, I looked down my nose at the negativity. Why did they drone on and on about their problems? Couldn't they reason themselves into agreement and love for each other? Shouldn't coming up with a common vision be simpler than this?

While we were busy trying to figure out our vision, relationships atrophied and tensions grew so high that more people began to leave. In the space of a few years, our already small group lost three families, whittling our numbers down from the forty who lived there when we moved to around twenty people.

After a few summers of Matthew managing the farm, it came to light that two of the farm workers, one of whom was a farm manager and also held a leadership position in the church, were meeting with a farm intern to exchange massages. While the intern assured us that the massages were consensual, several details about the massage sessions convinced us that ethical and professional boundaries had been crossed. Matthew was clear that this sort of behavior was not acceptable. The intern chose to leave, and Matthew bore the brunt of the relational fallout with the other two participants.

With these tensions simmering just below the surface, the farm seemed to be in danger of decaying. And relationships that had already been damaged by violated trust in the distant—and not so distant—past were decaying right along with it. This, along with a frightening encounter with a community visitor, led us to begin searching for a new job for Matthew and a place for us to move.

Our fragile idealism was bowing under the weight of decay and discord. Disillusionment was shaking the foundations of our life.

9

Interlude:
Saint Francis
and His Lady

*S*AINT FRANCIS is a hot mess. He has grown disil-
lusioned with his life. Merrymaking and money no
longer hold any interest for him. His friends, used to his
revelry, don't quite know what to do with their despondent
friend. They begin to titter and gossip behind his back: He's
no fun anymore! What is he rambling on about? Is he off in
the head? What a fool.

Francis takes refuge in a cavern in the mountains. He
spends hours and days praying mournful and penitent
prayers, sobbing for his past sins and for his days lost to
parties, women, and booze. For the violence and war for
which he thirsted in the name of noble knighthood. Day
after day, he returns to the cave for more penitence, "broken with fatigue and disfigured by sorrow,"[1] in the words

of one writer, and believing himself to be the greatest of all sinners.

After his repentant suffering is finally spent, his mourning eases and he emerges from the cave with a newfound joy and the feeling of God's goodness. The Lady of his dreams, who used to look like Saint George's princess—the archetype of the damsel in distress who needs rescuing—now turns out to be another kind of Lady entirely. Her identity might not be clear to him yet, but what is certain is that she is a Lady who inspires him. She will not leave him to his own devices.

With his newfound Ladylove in his heart, he takes a pilgrimage to Rome. Once there, this wealthy merchant's son—formerly decorated in shiny silks and the metal coat of a noble knight—mingles with beggars near Saint Peter's Basilica. He trades the sumptuous feasts of his father's table for their meager food.

On a ride through Assisi after his return from Rome, Francis is troubled again when he sees a leper. For all his prayers of penitence and confession, he is still repulsed by the pitiful sores of the sick. But instead of running from the repulsion the way he used to, Francis vows to follow the voice that spoke to him in his prayers in the cave:

> Francis! Everything which you have loved and desired in the flesh, it is your duty to despise and hate, if you wish to know my will. And when you have begun to do thus, all that which now seems to you sweet and lovely will become intolerable and bitter, but all which you used to avoid will turn itself to great sweetness and exceeding joy.[2]

When he sees the leper, he gets down off his horse and approaches the man. With trembling hands, he grasps the man's odorous, deformed flesh and brings the decaying hands to his own lips in a kiss.

Scales, like those of Saint George's dragon, fall from Francis's eyes. He sees a rip in the ether of reality. The once-muted colors crack until new colors whirl before him with beauty and life. Colors take on sweet taste and fragrance, and the world looks new to him.

Like Jesus' disciples—the tax collectors, zealots, cheats, and betrayers who drop everything to follow the Savior—Francis releases all the things he trusted in. When he finally embraces what once repulsed him, Francis's life becomes a simple undoing of everything he has depended on.

But his first efforts at releasing himself from the grip of greed and the seeking of empty pleasures aren't always well executed. Because Francis, in his commitment to poverty, feels such liberation from the yoke of his father's wealth, he is eager to share his freedom. But he preaches to a town that knows his history, that knows he is the son of a rich man. What can a rich kid teach about poverty? the towns-people wonder.[3]

And later, while praying in the dilapidated church of San Damiano, Francis has a profound and life-altering experience. He has a mystical vision. Hanging above the altar in the humble chapel, the crucifix begins to speak. "Francis, go and repair my house which, as you see, is falling into ruin."[4] When Christ speaks to him from the cross, exhilaration and purpose pound through Francis's body, and he rises to his feet. He will repair the church stone by stone if he must. What he doesn't yet realize is that Christ is speaking more broadly: Francis's task of transforming the small broken-down chapel will, in turn, transform the whole church.[5]

In the meantime, Francis realizes he needs money to re-pair the church. What better way to use his father's wealth than in the service of God?

So while Pietro is away, Francis breaks in and steals bolts of expensive cloth from his father's shop. He hurries away on horseback to another town, where he sells both the cloth and the horse. He returns to Assisi on foot and brings the money to the priest at San Damiano. Francis pleads with the priest to take the money for the decaying church. The priest knows Francis to be generous, but he also knows of his tendency to spend large amounts of money on parties. The priest figures out where this money has come from, and he refuses the treasure. Francis pleads that he has changed, and the priest eventually allows him to at least take refuge in the church.

Francis needs refuge because he knows what's coming. Francis has pushed his father too far.[6]

For weeks, Pietro searches for his son, the thief. While his father scours the countryside and sends out search parties, Francis hides and prays to God to save him. Eventually, he emerges, gaunt and thin and weak from hunger. He limps through the streets of Assisi, enduring the insults and torments of the countryfolk, who probably know what he's done.

When his father sees his son in the street, unrecognizable at first in dirt and rags, his response is savage. Pietro di Bernardone, his body hot with rage, bursts through the crowd to the beggar in their midst. He pounces on Francis, striking him so hard in the face that Francis stumbles. After more slaps and beatings, Pietro grabs Francis by the hair and drags him through the streets. Maybe his savagery riles up the crowd, whose anger bites at Francis's feet like the teeth of a wolf. Or maybe Pietro's fury, which one writer likens to an "instrument of the devil,"[7] is too brutal even for them.

Father and son enter the house of Bernardone in a twisting embrace of claw, hair, and fiery fury. Francis's mother, Pica, remembering the ring of fire that Francis brought at birth, reaches for her son. Pietro flings her back, and she stumbles against the wall. He is indeed possessed by something inhuman—or perhaps all *too* human. With one hand he holds his son, who is too weak to fight back, pulling out his hair in clumps. With the other hand, Pietro wraps heavy chains around his arm and pulls Francis into a closet. He beats Francis again and binds him with the chains. He spits on the pitiful figure of his bleeding son, then locks him away in the darkness.

He turns on Pica with quiet fury: "If you free him, I will treat you the same."

Pietro claims that these beatings are for Francis's own good—that the more uncomfortable he becomes, the more he will long for the riches and comfort with which he was raised. Pietro doesn't really understand his son or the conversion of his heart. What an irony for Francis, who has already begun to wear a hair shirt in his efforts at piety and confession.[8]

When Pietro leaves for another business trip, Pica speaks gently to Francis through the small hole in the door. "Your father is determined," she says. "He will not rest until you have apologized, relented, and returned to the store."

Francis doesn't respond. He murmurs prayers that stretch and bleed his lips, split from the beatings.

Pica stays with him, kneeling on the other side of the door and humming her French songs. They are the ones she sang to him when his fingers rested on the top of her breast as he nursed, the ones she sang to him when he brought her a wounded butterfly and begged her to heal it.

After hours of this, Francis suddenly begins to sing with his mother. She puts her hand on the old splintered door of his prison, and tears run down her face. When the song is done, the last one they will sing together, he calls to her: "Mother."

She shushes him gently as she stands, unhooks the key from its place beside the door, and opens the door for Francis. He flinches at the light streaming in and covers his bruised eyes with a dusty arm. Pica unlocks his chains, brings him some water, and gathers her skirts so she can lower to help him stand. He wobbles briefly, then takes her face in his hands.

"Father will be angry with you, Mother."

"Shush. That does not matter. He will yell and rage, but he would never really hurt me."

"The Lady calls to me, Mother," he says. "I cannot disappoint her."

"Which lady, my child?"

"You haven't seen her whom I love? You will."[9]

Even though this appears to be one of Francis's strange murmurings, Pica knows that he is utterly lucid now. He kisses her on each cheek and walks to the door. At the entrance, he pauses.

"She is Lady Poverty. And I will be true to her until I die."

With that, Francis leaves the house of Bernardone. And he never returns.

10

Letter to Saint Francis:
The Lunacy of Love

Dear Saint Francis,

I dreamed I saw the edge of your cloak slipping into the woods, and I wondered if you had found my first letter. If so, would you mind some more words from me?

At the risk of incurring your annoyance or disapproval, I am going to admit something to you: there are certain people (you among them) whom I'm really glad to see outside my window. And then there are others. Because I live in such an unusual situation, sometimes strangers tromp through my garden, allow their kids to play on the swing set my husband built for us; they become entirely too familiar with my backyard. Before I can remind myself that I own none of this beautiful land or my house, I wonder what right they have to be here. This is my space and my home, I think; go away!

Terrible, right? Not such saintly thoughts. But it's not only that. My stuff is overwhelming the space we have. I have too many things: standing before a closetful of clothes and knowing that our entire guest room floor is piled with laundry, I realize I'm failing at moving toward a lived simplicity. My heart is cluttered with the mess of my territorial materialism. Apparently, I've learned nothing from Jesus or you about simplicity. It is only a word, an idea that I can't seem to live out.

I mean, it's not as if I don't know, Francis, that simplicity is about more than just food and clothes. Clearly, those physical things are just tangible markers of our hearts. Which is what terrifies me. Is letting go of possessing and controlling my space, my things, my clothes, and even my family (as if they were extensions of my spirit)—is all this letting go supposed to make me feel adrift? Is letting go about being without identity and worth, about being alone and vulnerable, utterly helpless in the poverty of my spirit?

I long to follow you into the freedom of the simplicity you preached. That choice had repercussions in every part of your life. You were a misfit living in solidarity with those on the edges. As Franciscan friar and writer Richard Rohr has said, this made you truly "free to love."[1]

I want that freedom desperately. Sometimes I picture giving all my stuff away in some dramatic act of trust, as you did. Surely you stood in your father's shop and saw the colors of your life get bleaker and how the bolts of cloth seemed to bleed with the greed they were bought and sold with. When you decided, however ill-conceived, to steal your father's wealth to restore the chapel at San Damiano, did you stand in his shop for a moment, looking at all that meant so much to you—wealth, nobility, heroics, societal position? Did you feel that you had to ravage it all in order to move on?

When you finally left your father's house, your father complained to the bishop of Assisi, who summoned you, Francis, to his palace to answer for your sins against your father. It is said that the bishop told you: "You have scandalized your father. If you wish to serve God, return to him the money that you possess."[2]

To hear it told, your response shocked the bishop, the crowd, and your father. Removing first one piece of clothing, then another, you silenced the crowd by stripping yourself bare, naked of all the things your father possessed. On the floor lay also the painful hair shirt that you wore under your clothes, something that you would wear the rest of your life.[3]

It all sounds really dramatic and holy, but how does that work when you have a family? How do you give away everything when you have kids who need food, clothes for school, money for college, stability? This you might not understand, Francis. After all, you certainly weren't a mother or a wife. But one of the things that has most stripped me bare is motherhood. Although I do think it was gross when you kissed the sores of the leper, the truth is that most mothers (and thankfully, now many fathers) have come pretty close to that. From the moment our children are born we have our hands in their feces; we get puked on, peed on; we eat up the leftover food they've slobbered on.

Was that the miracle for you, Francis—that you were able to find intimacy with the suffering of the leper because you loved him as a parent loves his child, as God loves us, swapping spit, getting hands dirty?

Francis, when you stripped away each of your garments before the bishop until you were naked, is that when you took on simplicity? Your clothes were a symbol of the life you would lead: simple dress, simple living quarters, simple meals, and ultimately, the most simple of gospels: that God loves his children with a mad, mad love.

Francis, once you understood your need for this all-loving God, you didn't hesitate to strip naked in the way that God had already stripped your spirit in that cavern.

Ultimate simplicity is a willingness to give up not only all the material things that hinder us from following Jesus. Ultimate simplicity is giving up our very selves. This giving up of the self, writes one novelist, is "the ultimate form of wealth, and the most tyrannical."[4]

In a way, my closetful of clothes doesn't really matter. Or at least it's a symptom and not the cause of my heart trouble. Maybe simplicity, as it turns out, is both boringly simple and searingly difficult. True simplicity is about love—but in order to get there, I must take off my clothes. Not in a physical way, of course, but as a nudity of the heart. A chest, or even a body cavity, bared and raw, open to the elements, open to the sacred wounding that Christ endured.

When we endure these wounds ourselves, Christ is with us, sharing the burden of our suffering. All he asks is that we might let ourselves be overcome by the madness of a parent's love, a love that would lead us to kiss the festering wounds of another. That would lead us to the utter lunacy of God's love for us.

And that's worth giving up everything for.

Your simple friend,

Christiana

PART II

HOSPITALITY

*Once when I looked out the old farmhouse
window during an especially crowded time and
saw some footsore travelers coming along the road
and sighed, "I suppose they are coming here,"
one young worker said severely, "You should not
write the things you do unless you mean them."
In other words—do not write about hospitality
unless we are willing to assume the obligations
such writings bring with it.*

—Dorothy Day, *The Long Loneliness*

11

Strange Visitors

JAMES CAME BOUNDING through the heavy wooden door of the common building. It was right before church one Sunday morning in the middle of our fourth growing season. With his stained teeth, bleached hair, and funky floral shirt, James appeared to be an ex-hippie, a recovering addict, or both. He was an enthusiast, one who loved people, loved storytelling, and loved when people loved him back. With our flagging numbers, we all noticed and welcomed one extra person.

James felt free to chime in during our teaching time, offering up examples from his own life of working with the homeless and growing up in an Amish community. His stories were fascinating and sad: divorced parents who left the Amish, a sister who had ended up in a messianic cult, a son from a previous relationship, a radio show where he interviewed the likes of musician Jennifer Knapp.

James spent his days helping on the farm with Matthew. Matthew lent James his old computer to use in the apartment he was staying in up the hill. We welcomed him into our home for meals. Since our family had expanded to include a son named Jude, James spent some time reading to our small children and talked about his own young son, who lived with his ex-wife. He talked about his upbringing in an Amish community and answered our questions about the quirks of such a life.

A few things were odd, though. James said he was keeping a blog about his time with us, and when I found it online, he had posted pictures of actual Amish folks and labeled them "Plow Creekers." When Matthew asked him about it, James was quick to say that he and his editor had miscommunicated and it would be fixed. I didn't quite believe him.

But since moving to Plow Creek, my instincts and my perceptions had shifted, and I put it out of my mind. In some ways my shifting perceptions were good. Just as Francis struggled with being able to approach the leper with compassion, I had to work to not dismiss new acquaintances because my perceptions of them were based on my own biases and prejudices. My younger self would have been outwardly kind to a man like James but would have kept him at arm's length.

To me, James seemed overly eager to share interesting stories. And I could tell he'd lived a rough life. I was trying, in my way, to accept someone whom my instincts told me to steer clear of. I was trying to be open to hospitality even when it made me uncomfortable.

One evening, Matthew received an email from a woman who said she was James's sister, Polly—the sister who'd been involved in a messianic cult. Polly wrote that their mother had died and that she hadn't been able to reach James: Could Matthew have her brother contact her?

Matthew, who was wondering at this point how to tell a new acquaintance that his mother had died, called another man from the community. Together they went to give James the news.

James reacted as one might expect when you hear your mother has died suddenly: tears, questions, deep emotion. But something didn't ring quite true. Why would a woman trapped in a messianic cult email her brother? Why would she have Matthew's email address and not her brother's?

In a lull during the exchange, Matthew went to fetch the computer he had lent to James. He discovered that James had recently created an email address—the very email address from which "Polly" had sent the message about his mother's death.

At nearly the same time, while sitting at home and feeling strange about the whole thing, I began to search the Internet. Buried in the latter pages of a Google search, I found an online article about James that was several years old. The article, from a web page that looked part blog and part sketchy advertising website, described James caring for his ailing father *after his mother's death*.

When Matthew went back to confront James, our visitor grew defensive, and the cracks that we'd already observed widened. It was clear that he'd invented the story about his mother and probably many more details of his life. Who knew if Polly or the Amish upbringing ever existed?

Matthew returned home late in the evening to relay the whole story to me. I panicked. All my personal boundary alarms, the ones which I'd hushed in order to show hospitality to James, were sounding at their highest volumes. Though he'd never given us any indication that he was violent, I was terrified. What if, in anger and retribution, James came down the hill in the middle of the night and slaughtered us all?

To allay my fears, Matthew slept in the hallway. Thankfully, James stayed away that night, and we were physically safe. The next day, James was driven to the bus station and given a one-way ticket back to his home state (if that really was his home state).

But something was closing up inside of me. This was not the first time our ideals of hospitality had been tested, and I felt myself curling back inwards, wanting to pull my family back into its secure unit, safe from the messiness of other people.

* * *

One summer afternoon a few weeks before James arrived, Matthew had called me from the field.

"Would you be okay if I brought a couple over for lunch?"

"Sure," I said. "I can stretch it. Who are they?"

Though his explanation was rushed, Matthew relayed as much as he could over the phone. Our guests had been dropped off at the Plow Creek field by a police officer. He had responded to several complaints that a suspicious couple was walking down the road a few towns over. I'm not sure if we should've been pleased or offended that Plow Creek, with our crew of misfits, was the first place he thought to bring them.

Matthew was alone in the field when the police officer approached him with the couple. Matthew agreed to host them, and the cop left.

I was excited to be hosting our first quirky pilgrims. Wasn't this what Jesus called us to do: welcome the stranger? When Matthew walked into the house with the couple, he introduced them to me.

"This is Abraham and Sarah," he said.

I suppressed a giggle and knew that in order to maintain my composure, I'd have to avoid looking at Matthew directly. Seriously? Abraham and Sarah? Like the Hebrew couple who welcomed strangers long ago—strangers who turned out to be God and his angels? Had I been a better person, I may have found the biblical connection rich with meaning.

Instead, I was trying very hard not to laugh.

As we sat down to lunch, I noticed that Sarah was quite a bit older than Abraham, who looked to be in his mid-twenties. She began to serve Abraham and cut his food for him.

At first I thought that maybe our guests were on a pilgrimage, something that some of our neighbors had done years before, setting off on a trip the way Jesus had sent out his disciples: without money, food, or a change of clothes, praying that God would provide. It was a strange concept to someone raised in a state where that kind of pilgrimage could mean death by heat, highway traffic, or someone with a loose trigger finger. But I was at least familiar with the concept. We began to try to relate to Abraham and Sarah with our own concept of pilgrimage, asking them about where they came from and where they were going.

But the usual pleasantries of conversation were quickly replaced with something else. It turned out that Abraham and Sarah were on less of a pilgrimage and more of a mission to convert others. When we noticed the conversation turning, we tried to relate, letting them know that we were Christians and they didn't need to proselytize us. But we weren't the right kind of followers of God for our guests.

Halfway through the meal, it became clear to our guests that we were not willing to adhere to their gospel. I suppose they could've shaken the dust off their feet and left. Instead, Sarah grew angry at us, and Matthew suggested that he take them to the nearest bus station. Sarah and Abraham got up from the table abruptly and walked out to Matthew's truck, grumbling, and without so much as a word of thanks.

The strange encounter with Abraham and Sarah was followed by yet another. One evening, we invited a couple in their fifties over for dinner. They were visiting the community and had all their belongings in their Jeep. The woman was as submissive and timid as her husband was chatty. The soup had hardly been ladled when he began to explain to us how our community wasn't radical enough, that we weren't really living the gospel, and that we were trapped in complacency.

"For instance," he said, "Paul says that we who are in Christ Jesus are free from sin. See, I think when you get to a certain age, you just don't sin anymore." He glanced at his wife. "I don't sin. Do I?"

This time, I couldn't suppress a laugh when I saw her expression. Her submissiveness didn't keep her from showing the fact that she did not share his views on his lack of sin.

Matthew or I mumbled something about pride being a sin. But clearly, the heart of the conversation was over. After dinner, the couple headed out to their vehicle and drove off to the next intentional community. Even now, I wonder if they are driving around the countryside in their Jeep, still searching for the perfect place to fit their ideals.

* * *

After James left, Matthew and I took the kids to a hotel for the weekend. We needed to get away and reevaluate. In my idealism, I had tried to be radical in my hospitality. I had prided myself that we welcomed strangers into our home.

But after James, we felt naïve, unprotected, and angry that someone had duped us so easily. I began to feel hostile to the idea of hospitality in general. I wondered if we should allow strangers into our home anymore. I felt wounded by rudeness, fear, lies, and odd ideas.

Perhaps Sarah had been right; perhaps I did need to be converted. But just not in the way she thought.

12

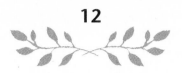

Interlude:
The Do-Gooder

*F*OR MANY YEARS, Mennonites have been known to be in the trenches, both literally and metaphorically, doing hard and sometimes tragic work for the kingdom. Taking a stand against fighting war, many went to war-torn areas and worked for peace. They were involved in many organizations, both Mennonite and otherwise, that reached out to the marginalized in the United States and overseas. So it's no surprise that after a few years among radical Mennonites, I began to hear about a particular organization that was involved with housing the homeless, something called the Catholic Worker. And the name I kept hearing associated with the Catholic Worker Movement, a name spoken in reverent tones reserved for saints, was Dorothy Day.

Dorothy Day was a practical mystic for the twentieth century, a Catholic anarchist, a privileged girl in her youth who chose poverty as an adult, a woman acquainted with her own brokenness who took in and loved the broken-hearted. The humble flickers of the Catholic Worker's beginnings in the early parts of the twentieth century have flared out into hundreds of communities, still vibrantly serving the most marginalized even today.

Much like Francis, Dorothy, even before her conversion to Catholicism, showed signs in both her life and personality of what she would later become. In the same way that Francis's boyhood generosity followed him into adulthood, Dorothy's time with the marginalized before her conversion continued after it. She was always drawn to the people whom no one else noticed, and she wondered what kind of lives they led: the street sweeper, the subway attendant, the minister off duty.

Like Francis, Dorothy mourned some mistakes of her youth when she became a converted Catholic and found them difficult to talk about later in life. And like the saint, her past mistakes and suffering gave her a large measure of compassion and empathy and a feeling of responsibility for what she should accomplish.

* * *

Dorothy Day is born in 1897 to a middle-class family in New York City. By all accounts, her childhood is, if not perfect, at least as comforting and safe as Francis's—though her father isn't as boorish as his. She spends a good part of her youth in Chicago and attends the University of Illinois in Urbana as a college student. There her social justice leanings become pronounced; she runs in Socialist crowds and becomes interested in journalism. Her writing grows increasingly radical, and she is drawn to those who are suffering. At the same time, she becomes an active part of the New York intellectual scene, befriending famous artists and writers of the time.

In her twenties, she has a fling, becomes pregnant, and then has an abortion, something that will haunt her after she becomes a Catholic. She will come to regret the abortion, even as she remains reluctant to talk about it and uneasy about judging others' choices. She has a short-lived marriage, and she is involved in peaceful protests for women's right to vote, which gets her arrested and lands her in jail several times.

As with Francis's experiences in prison, these days in jail are powerful moments for her. In his book *Dorothy Day: A Radical Devotion*, Robert Coles says that while in jail, Dorothy feels "the degradation of the jailers as well as the jailed." In prison, her encounters with prostitutes and petty thieves move and sadden her.[1] She reads the Psalms in those days of confinement and, despite her lack of certainty about faith and God, finds herself drawn to prayer.

In her late twenties, Dorothy begins a relationship with Forster Batterham, an atheist, scientist, and anarchist. Although they have very different views of God, they are happy for several years and enter into a common-law marriage. Then they have a child together named Tamar Teresa. The tension between Forster and Dorothy becomes too much to overcome as she moves toward Catholicism and decides to baptize Tamar. Forster doesn't understand or approve of Dorothy's desire to connect with God, but she finds herself inexorably drawn to faith. When Dorothy decides to be baptized into the Roman Catholic Church herself, her relationship with Forster finally begins to unravel.

But Dorothy Day's writings are full of compassion for Forster. When she joins the Catholic Church, it is God, and not Forster, who becomes her first lover, her beloved. And Forster cannot fathom this conversion. Dorothy writes: "Why should not Forster be jealous? Any man who did not participate in this love would, of course, realize my infidelity, my adultery."[2]

Like the conversion of Saint Francis, Dorothy's conversion leads her to her greatest Love. In his exuberant and dramatic way, Francis calls his new love Lady Poverty. Dorothy says, "I loved the Church for Christ made visible."[3]

Eventually, Dorothy moves to New York City with Tamar. A few years later, a quirky middle-aged Frenchman—who is known to speak in riddles and repetitive free verse—walks into her life. Peter Maurin could be Saint Francis himself; he is a man Dorothy Day calls a "troubadour of God"[4] (one of Francis's nicknames). Though he loves to speak to his flock of misfit followers, Peter never tries to gather people around him. What he really desires is for them to be drawn in by the truth of his message: justice, care for the poor, and the availability of good food.[5]

Peter's passion for justice and for the poor gives great direction to Dorothy's life and work. She longs for her faith and life to be in deep harmony. Dorothy sees that Peter himself is already living his faith through his lifestyle of scarcity. "How glowing a thing it is in Franciscan literature, and how many illusions people have about it!" she writes. "But Peter *lived* it. He literally possessed nothing."[6]

When Peter Maurin approaches Dorothy, he wants her to partner with him in three things: to provide a place for discussion, to create houses of hospitality, and to build up farming communes to provide food for the poor.

To fulfill the need for what Peter calls "round-table discussion," Dorothy and her friends put together a magazine, the *Catholic Worker*, often sold for a cent on street corners by those left unemployed or homeless by the Great Depression. Their magazine provides an intellectual look at poverty and the suffering of the marginalized. The folks who gather in the *Catholic Worker*'s tiny offices and garden space in the "slum section of New York City," as it is then known, eventually grow this magazine into the second thing Peter dreamed of: hospitality houses for those without homes, food, or jobs.[7]

Dorothy and her friends live alongside the poor in these houses, befriending and sharing with them in their joys and suffering. In her book *Loaves and Fishes*, Dorothy tells story after story of the men, women, and children she meets who are struggling to live during the Great Depression: immigrants, veterans, single mothers, the elderly with no place to go, the mentally ill and unstable, the mean, the thieves, the lonely, and the sick. It seems that there is no one they won't accept or befriend, even if they cannot be housed because of the overwhelming need.

Soon the work of Dorothy Day and Peter Maurin spreads. Soon autonomously run houses of hospitality are popping up across the country. Soon Peter is ready for his third dream to become a reality: communitarian farms.

But the reality of farm life will turn out to be quite different from the dream.

13

Dream Home

*A*FTER THE DISQUIET and the stress of the farm and strange visitors, Matthew began to look for jobs, mostly unrelated to farming. We decided that after a few years in intentional community, we'd had our challenging adventure. Now it was time to start dreaming of our new, ideal life somewhere else. Where could we live that would make us the most satisfied and could give our kids the most diverse experiences and the best schooling? Where could we have the most beautiful life? What would make us happy?

We explored the idea of living closer to one of our families, which meant Texas, Missouri, or a state in between. We looked online and occasionally in person at houses and land in many of these places, wondering what kind of job Matthew could take in the city. He researched becoming a firefighter, revisited his teaching days, and applied for an office job that ran large organic farms. We knew that our ability to even have a conundrum about where we should live was a privilege. Still, it was also a great source of anxiety.

When Matthew's job search grew frustrating, we wondered whether farming on our own might perhaps be the best vocation for our family.

I began to dream of a beautiful farmhouse with an expansive kitchen, with two or more bathrooms, my own laundry room, and a garden with a clothesline. With this picture in mind, I was on my way toward dreaming up our new life. It wasn't long before we found our perfect homestead.

One spring, we drove up north to look at farms for sale. Near a small village, up on a hill in the beautiful Driftless region of Wisconsin, was a large-acreage farm put on the market by an older couple who was ready to downsize. As we drove up the steep driveway on the property, we passed over a creek. I could imagine our children, Neva and Jude, playing in the stream and climbing the trees in the small apple orchard adjacent to the farmhouse.

Along with his Amish neighbor who helped him in the fields, the farmer was waiting for us in the barn. While Matthew took a tour of the land, the wife of the farmer ushered me and our small children into their kitchen. She was an elegant and intellectual woman, and she extolled the beauties of living in the region. She told me about the local community and the neighboring farms.

She had recently refurbished their open kitchen with antique wood cabinetry, and blue Spanish tiles she'd bought in Texas lined the backsplash of the kitchen. The Texas connection felt like a sign.

Their first living room overlooked part of the farm down the hill, and the second held a piano. There were four bedrooms, two bathrooms, a laundry room, and a basement. Next to the farmhouse was a small guesthouse that had been housing their Amish neighbors, who worked for them. One room in the guesthouse was lined with shelves of their canned goods. Directly beside the guesthouse was a hammock and clothesline and a lovely kitchen garden. The farmer dug a shovel into the earth to demonstrate the depth of the dark, rich topsoil.

"I think I've found my dream home," I said to Matthew as we drove away hours later.

"I think I've found my dream farm," he replied.

So we started the process of applying for a loan for the farm, which was rather expensive. Emotionally, I began to leave Plow Creek behind. Our conversations in those days surrounded that farm in Wisconsin. How could we use the guesthouse? Where would Matthew buy farming equipment? How would our neighbors respond to our arrival? Where would we go to church? I even mentally arranged our furniture into the farmhouse, thinking of what new pieces we would need to fill the space. I wondered what kind of flowers I would plant in the garden, and how far the nearest airport was that could get us to our families.

Just when our dream was making itself at home in our imaginations, we heard the bad news: we didn't qualify for a loan.

Like a thunderous wave, the doors of those barns and farmhouse were slammed in our faces.

That fall, with no job in sight and no ideas for a perfect place to move, Matthew recommitted to another farm season.

14

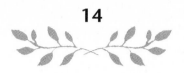

Interlude:
Commune Farms

*I*N THE 1930s, Dorothy Day continues to pursue Peter Maurin's dream, one that has also become her own. His dream is that a communitarian farm and agronomic university can provide solutions to the suffering that they are encountering. Through their houses of hospitality, Dorothy and Peter are living close to a variety of social problems, which she identifies as "unemployment, delinquency, destitute old age, man's rootlessness, lack of room for growing families, and hunger."[1]

Their first attempt is an acreage in Staten Island so small that they begin to call it a "garden commune" instead of a farm. These first farming experiences are fraught with conflicts between the ones whom Dorothy calls the "workers" and the "scholars": those who come to farm the land versus those who are there to learn from Peter Maurin's "agronomic university."[2] The two groups can't understand one another, and they—like many of the other different kinds of folks who come to live or work at the garden commune—bring their troubles with them. Even those who offer well-intentioned or creative solutions to various problems often end up making more work for others. One man, a recovering addict, wants to save money on coal by collecting driftwood for the furnace. But the wood is so wet that it dampens the fires, which then take more work to restart. As Dorothy says, every person who visits and works in the community sees "the commune in terms of his own desires."[3]

The younger people build their hopes on dreams of more space and land for crops and animals. With a substantial donation from a young teacher who wants to live on the property, Dorothy gives in to pressure and sells the farm on Staten Island to buy another, larger farm in Pennsylvania. They name it Maryfarm, and the farm commune is born.

But Maryfarm is burdened with even more conflict than their first attempt at farming. One man named Maurice, who lives for many years at Maryfarm, is, according to Dorothy, "like many old men . . . a terror."[4] Maurice takes delight in comparing every woman he meets to the mother who raised him and his twenty siblings, and they never live up to his mother's version of womanhood (adept at nursing, baking, sewing). When Maurice himself begins to refuse food from the communal kitchen, he also starts to tell short-term visitors that he is never given any food.

In response, when the guests leave, they send back provisions of food, alms, and even clothing for poor Maurice. Dorothy wonders: "What must they think of us, whom he accused so constantly of neglecting?"[5]

Their farm, open to absolutely anyone who wants to be there, creaks and groans under the pressure of the disparate needs and desires of so many.

15

Frustrations and Celebrations

*D*OROTHY DAY'S commune farm was not the only farm to have its workers and residents impose their own desires and expectations. The truth is, we all imposed our own expectations on life in community. When we moved to Plow Creek, I hoped to live among other parents with children, to have lots of help with childcare, to share more of our life together. But it took years at Plow Creek to have anything approximating a community of parents, mainly because there were few other children our kids' ages.

Similarly, our farming interns often committed to the farm season with unarticulated expectations of their own. As a whole, our interns were hard-working, fun-loving, and a vibrant addition to the community. But it was no surprise that some of them would view the farm the way we had when we moved. It seemed to them an idyllic way to spend a summer: learning gardening, selling at farmers' markets, herding goslings, playing with chicks and piglets, writing in their journals, and reading Wendell Berry in the evenings.

But when one monotonous hour after another was spent bent over, weeding strawberries in the high heat of summer; when farmers' markets required spending a slow Saturday under a tent in the sun; when work hours meant you sometimes had to get up before six in the morning; when you were tired from lifting watermelons or riding your bike a mile back to the field to do a chore you'd forgotten and then climbing the steep trail back up to your apartment on the hill: well, unexpressed expectations began to surface.

Farm work was exhausting. And early on, I stopped feeling guilty that I didn't enjoy it or have the physical stamina for it. I was content with cooking, preserving, and taking care of my own little messy garden outside my house. But from my kitchen window that looked out on some of the spaces they occupied, I empathized with the interns—a few of whom would rather be reading about farming than actually doing it—as the heat, hard work, and isolation caught up with many of them. Many struggled to finish the season. And some of them didn't.

Early in our years on the farm, before Matthew understood that the intern program was weak, some of the interns left before the season was over. During his third farm season, three out of the four interns left early. One intern left without much of a goodbye, leaving many of his things behind. Another young woman in her early twenties, stressed by spiritual and physical exhaustion, left early as well.

Two farm seasons after the inappropriate massages between two of the farm workers, (one of whom was a manager) and an intern, the same manager once again crossed boundaries. Now the raw and unaddressed tensions on the farm boiled over. Now, without strong leadership in the community to hold people accountable and help the community process the stresses, the tensions between the members of the farm team became nearly unbearable.

* * *

Just as those interns had expectations of farm work, I had my own expectations of hospitality. Some of them percolated in my imagination, but I hadn't been able to articulate them: Won't I feel good when we open our home, even to people who are different than we are? Won't we all learn from each other, and all barriers will be broken down in a holy communion of love and neighborliness?

I think my ideals were good. The visitors during our first years in community led me to question my naïve ideals about hospitality and my childish views of love for one's neighbor. But as we lived longer in community and experienced the often chaotic, stressful happenings, I felt an unpleasant sense that the hostility I was feeling toward our guest James extended not only to strangers in our community but to some of my community neighbors as well.

Where Dorothy Day's Maurice was a terror, our community neighbors offered different kinds of challenges. I wouldn't call them terrors, but a few of them were very challenging to live with. But the truth is that I only experienced the tensions, at least on the farm, secondhand. I was appalled when Matthew told me what was going on at work, and we got into the habit of talking about these events all the time.

It became an unpleasant pastime: he would come home after a frustrating day, he would vent or I would ask about it, and we'd spend hours hashing and rehashing, making each other and ourselves more and more angry. After years of this, Matthew made the comment that sometimes he spent more time thinking about the tensions of the farm and the challenging people he worked with than he did thinking about his own children. Truthfully, Matthew wasn't alone in this. I regret my immaturity in handling some of these situations. I know I could have been more loving.

When leadership flounders in a community—especially when that community is skeptical of authority anyway—the insecurities, tensions, and anxieties in all of us emerge into the light. Misshapen and wounded pieces of ourselves surface from within, and we must examine, acknowledge, and deal with them—or bleed all over ourselves and everyone else.

I think that's what happened with the tensions on the farm, and with the old trauma that still created discord, even years afterward. The relaxed expectations from the years after Conrad left were a good balance when the ethos was too harsh and overreaching, but the pendulum began to swing in the other direction. The "live and let live" ethos of the community was catching up to us. Unclear boundaries in community led to confusion and tension, and I sometimes felt bitter against my neighbors; I spoke about them unkindly. Our sins and weaknesses emerged in the thicket of chaos, and without the support of the community, the farm seemed as if it might implode.

Frankly, I think I was more willing to extend hospitality to the stranger than to my own brothers and sisters in Christ. In my community, strangers and visitors were not usually permanent. We could present to them our best selves for a while—offering good meals, clean beds, and unchallenging conversation. But even if those visitors were unpleasant or offered strange experiences, like James, in the end, they would leave. And once the shock wore off, at least we had good stories to tell.

But to live beside others day after day, to be confronted with their flaws and to be shamed by our own, to offer love amid continual hurt or annoyance: this was another challenge and another kind of hospitality. One that was easier to talk about than actually live.

* * *

After our attempts to move to our dream home were thwarted, Matthew and I eventually settled back into life at Plow Creek. Even if the drama hadn't completely faded, the community was at least in a healthier place. After Matthew expressed the need for support when conflicts arose, the community used the downtime between growing seasons to restructure. Going forward, a team of community members would help Matthew and the other manager oversee the work.

Matthew and I began to mend from the fear and pain of those strange and scary visitors like James; we started to yearn for more complex and radical ways of showing hospitality. We wanted to see things with joyful eyes instead of the division that seemed to mark most of the areas of our life. Even as the population of the community dwindled and tensions lingered, we saw that the members of our community longed to care for each other. Celebration became a means by which we could draw from our gifts, both personally and as a community. We managed to show hospitality through festivals, feasts, worship services, and, for one family, through foster care.

The summer's busyness peaked in mid-June during the Strawberry Festival, one of the long-term collaborations Plow Creek had forged with the nearby village, which hosted the event in front of the local museum. The Friday evening before the festival, we capped and sliced strawberries as a community, laughing together and singing hymns as the red juice of the berries dripped down our wrists. The next morning we took turns serving strawberry shortcake to customers at the festival while the farm team bustled back and forth between the field and town, selling strawberries and vegetables and managing U-pick back at the field two miles away.

On two different occasions, summer brought former farm interns who chose to be married in the meadow. Barn dances, bluegrass bands, and vows spoken under the shade of the willow tree filled us with hope for the future.

Then in early fall, when the fireflies still peppered the dusky evenings with light, we invited those beyond our intentional community—people from the village and another nearby Mennonite church—to join in our harvest festival. Harvesting had become to us a cherished symbol of the fruit of faithfulness and hard work and our ability to push through the many challenges of community. We celebrated all that the farm had accomplished over the season and the strides we had managed to make in our communal life together.

Childlike silliness reigned. Adults competed in pudding-eating and marshmallow "chubby bunny" contests on picnic tables at the edge of the meadow. While the kids colored and made crafts under the willow tree, their parents had lawn game tournaments a few yards away. I fashioned a giant bubble wand from sticks, rope, and dishwashing liquid, and even the adults were transfixed by the way reality seemed to twist and shift inside the layers of water and soap molecules. Our children leapt at the shivering prisms that sometimes reached lengths of eight feet, and they felt in equal measures elated and disappointed when the giant bubbles popped.

Then, when winter cloaked the earth in white and all our vegetables and fruits were tucked neatly into jars and gallon-sized freezer bags, we shifted back into the stillness of the resting season. The cold forced us to stop our physical labors, and the early darkness sent us to our beds. As Advent approached, we decorated the worship space with festive banners, garlands, and glass bells that an elderly member had made many years before. We sang "O Come, O Come, Emmanuel" in a candlelit service and waited. Waited. Waited in the hope of new birth.

We wondered if more people would join our ragtag group of misfits. We trusted the faithfulness of our older members, who had lived through the ebb and flow of decades in such a longstanding community. More would come, we trusted, and God would be faithful.

One evening, our neighbors Matt and Angela, who'd been vetted for the foster care system, told us that they had gotten a call from their social workers. A sister and brother needed a place to stay. Once Matt and Angela brought them home, it didn't take long for their new kids to befriend our own. Soon, the house beat to the drumming of little shoes running back and forth through the doors of our shared laundry room into our adjoining apartments; the children batted at the winter blues with laughter and became more like siblings than friends.

Hope was being nurtured, and we wondered if the gift of these children was the beginning of new life in our community.

Matt and Angela had the kids for a few months, and then a family member from out of state moved closer to reunify their family. We were heartbroken for Matt and Angela when they said farewell to the children who had enriched all our lives. For months, our son Jude, who was only just beginning to speak in full sentences, asked faithfully where his best friend was.

It was a painful question for Matt and Angela—they wondered where the children were, too, and if they were thriving.

And then, one day, nine months later, when Jude asked Angela where his friend was, she was able to tell him that he was returning. Angela and Matt were entrusted with the children's care again, and this time it would be permanent. The kids all picked up right where they had left off, and our doors were once again swinging open for the exuberant strangers who had become family.

16

Letter to Dorothy Day:
A Saint for Difficult People

Dear Dorothy,

Can I tell you something peculiar?[1] I've been writing letters to Saint Francis of Assisi, talking to him as if he might write me back, imagining he would tell me how I might keep from failing at simplicity.

As I sat down to write to you, hoping that you too could have something to teach me, I found that the writing was both more difficult and a little less strange than writing to the troubadour. You died a few years after I was born, so at the very least, you technically could have held me in your arms as a baby. I think that makes you seem more real to me. Your life is full of provable history instead of the mess of Saint Francis's story: part truth, part hagiography, and part legend, all things that I could romanticize.

Your story is grittier because of its relationship to reality.

When I think of you, two images come to mind. In a black-and-white photo, you are older, seated among a crowd of standing police officers, guns at their hips. With your wide-brimmed hat and your hands clasped in front of your knees, you might as well be sitting at the beach: you look at peace with protest and conflict. At other times, I picture you as a painting, in an icon by a Franciscan brother named Robert Lentz: your face golden but slightly sad, lined by years of suffering with others. The painting doesn't quite capture your noble beauty. But the Austrian girl braid you often wore when your hair was grey and a copy of the *Catholic Worker* are present. Gold leaf is a backsplash behind you, and there is a thin red line circling your head.

There have already been calls to canonize you. You are being numbered among the beloved mystics you wrote about: Saint Francis, Saint John of the Cross, Teresa of Ávila, and Catherine of Siena. I suppose you would respond to this the way you've responded before: "Don't call me a saint. I don't want to be dismissed so easily."[2]

Despite your grumpiness about it, the church just might ignore your wishes. But don't take it too hard; I think you being a saint could be good for many people. I recently read an article about you called "A Saint for Difficult People."[3] You might guess that my first thoughts were about all the difficult people I've lived with in community: people who have challenged, frustrated, and annoyed me. People who seem a little like the Maurice you write about in *Loaves and Fishes*, or the racist Mr. Breen whom you allowed to live in one of your houses of hospitality. Those parts of your writing resonated with me, because you knew the struggle of trying to love those who didn't know how to feel loved.

Sometimes I take comfort in the words of Henri Nouwen. In his book *Reaching Out*, he talks about hospitality as a sort of spectrum. He suggests that in order to journey from hostility to hospitality, its opposite pole, we have to admit "our own hostilities and fears without hesitation."[4]

But, Dorothy, I confess to you who knows more about hospitality than most people: I'm not good at this kind of loving. I've tried. I really have, but sometimes I feel stuck in the hostility part. The daily discipline of loving my neighbor is often ugly and painful. In larger churches, people don't have to face these unpleasant people every day. Once we are home, we take the memory of them off as we shed our Sunday dress. But intentionally nurturing neighborly love means recognizing that this love cannot be taken off.

I want to practice love and hospitality the way you did. But I feel so inadequate.

Before I moved to this community, my view of hospitality was of the societal kind, meaning the hospitality that is taught in home economics classes or by Miss Manners, in *Martha Stewart Living* and *Better Homes and Gardens*. It is the hospitality of cleanliness, order, color, and beauty.

This facet of hospitality can be lovely. It can be the gift of an artist who uses her talents to express abundance and creativity. I have witnessed and been the recipient of such gorgeous details, and I know that they can be filled with beauty and charity. I love setting out my grandmother's china and linens for Christmas parties or baby showers that bring joy to others. But for me, the harder hospitality is the daily dirtiness—both literal and metaphorical—of allowing others into your home and spaces when they aren't lovely.

Once, a friend of mine came over with her own baby in tow so that two desperate women could share their desperation. I was awash with shame because I had gotten the date wrong. I thought she was coming a week later. My hair was a mess, my house was a wreck, I wasn't wearing a bra, I had breast milk dripping down the inside of my shirt, and I was anxious and suffering from postpartum depression. My friend was gracious, and told me that she was glad I was so real. But the truth is, if I'd known she was coming, I wouldn't have been quite *that* real. I would have cleaned up my house, swept the floor, brushed my hair, put on a bra, and organized the mudroom.

This is a metaphor for me. Hospitality is about offering your heart and home when it isn't clean or even convenient— when your house feels full already and one more child, one more knock on the door, one more neighbor asking you for something, feels as if it will break you apart. That's the dirty trick of it all and why so many of us shy away: because this kind of hospitality is about offering who we really are, revealing our whole, real selves: the good, the bad, and the dirty.

When my neighbors Matt and Angela opened their lives by taking in a young sister and brother from the foster care system, they were showing hospitality. They completely embraced the griefs of their children. But the truth is that their hospitality opened up not only their lives to being changed but all of ours as well. Not only were Matt and Angela changed; our whole community was changed by the children's presence.

Howard Thurman, an African American mystic-prophet, writing in the 1940s, noted that the missionary stance can lead to self-righteousness. If we approach hospitality only as the hosts, as the helpers and heroes, then we are in the position of power. We risk turning hospitality into something less like a relationship and more like charity.

Maybe that's the heart of it, Dorothy. It takes humility to be changed by the people who come into our lives. We show them our dirty houses and our weaknesses, we take on their sorrows as our own, and we open ourselves up to the things we can learn from them. True hospitality means that I let others change me too.

But as for the most difficult people among us? As I think about it now, perhaps it's true that you are a saint for those "difficult people" in my community. And perhaps then you are also the perfect saint for me too.

Your difficult friend,

Christiana

PART III

CONTEMPLATION

Place your mind in the mirror of eternity;
place your soul in the splendor of glory;
place your heart in the figure of the divine substance;
and, through contemplation, transform your entire
being into the image of the Divine One himself,
so that you too may experience what his friends
experience when they taste the hidden sweetness that
God alone has kept from the beginning
for those who love him.

—Saint Clare of Assisi, "Third Letter to Agnes"

17

Winter

I THOUGHT I WAS becoming well acquainted with the way the seasons swept in upon us year after year: the sloshing of mud season in early April that gave way to the beloved rebirth of spring, the growing season that ended with a few weeks of summer heat that were just miserable enough to make us glad when the Asian beetles accompanied the changing colors of autumn. But my Texas constitution, so in awe of snow the first few years, began to balk at the bitter approach of winter. The season's chill and dormancy only pressed upon me physically in the beginning years; the cold caused some annoyance and discomfort of the body. But eventually, winter would begin to evoke pain and darkness for my whole self, as it pressed upon not just my body but my mind and spirit too.

I went into labor with our second child, Jude, on a cold night in December, a blizzard on the horizon. In the days leading up to the birth, I began to notice quiet glances between Matthew and my mother. They were concerned about the weather. But to make light of their shared worry, they began a running joke between them that Matthew should keep the John Deere tractor warmed up in case we needed to use it to get to the hospital during a blizzard. The hospital was forty minutes away, after all, and the winter was our harshest yet.

Oddly enough, I wasn't worried. Maybe it was because a woman had already given birth in my backyard and I knew I would have Angela's help if I needed to have the baby at home. But perhaps it was also because I'd already begun the inward turning that comes with the discomfort of late pregnancy. My body had begun to recall the pain of giving birth to Neva, preparing for the concentrated breathing that would bring this baby into the world. My mother wondered aloud if God let the end of the third trimester be so miserable because otherwise a woman afraid of childbirth or motherhood might be content to keep that baby tucked up in her warm womb indefinitely.

But I was miserable enough that I was ready to give birth. And the tractor wasn't necessary when I first began to have labor pains. There was no blizzard, only snow that had settled so comfortably in its place that it was a wonder it could ever be persuaded to leave.

On our initial drive to the hospital, we got stuck for fifteen minutes at a railroad crossing, waiting for the seemingly endless stream of ethanol cars to pass. And when we finally arrived, Matthew, my mother, and I were sequestered in a hospital room so cold that we had to ask repeatedly for more blankets to put against the window frames. Eventually, the labor stalled, and they sent me home the next morning. Our car doors were frozen shut, and the negative-degree chill was almost enough to take my mind off the disappointment of still being in one piece instead of two.

A week later, the weather was only slightly warmer when I went back to the hospital. We were in the same hospital room as we'd been in on that cold night. This time, my mom had come prepared; she'd brought along a space heater.

I had told my midwife repeatedly, in the weeks leading up to the birth and even when I first arrived at the hospital, that I wanted to use a hypnobirthing labor technique. When it was time for the birth, instead of pushing, I would breathe the baby down the birth canal, oh so gently.

But when the transition came, I was standing up, cursing and shaking so badly that I could barely register the midwife's urgings for me to slow down, to breathe him out. Instead, I pushed the baby out fast and hard, almost too quickly for the midwife to catch him before he hit the floor. She handed him up to me and I sank onto the bed.

As I settled back with this new boy in my arms, I wondered at his resemblance to his big sister. He looked familiar. Was it the protruding chin from my side of the family, his dark, full head of hair so much like my own at birth? Or did I see myself not only in his features but also in the pulsing of our shared blood under the thin skin of his cheeks?

When the nurse finally put him on the scale, we both gasped at the weight. I had formed and birthed a nine-pound baby boy.

Two days later, we drove Jude home with snow falling in that sort of sideways way that feels Alice-in-Wonderland-like, as if the sky has cocked its head to the side.

No, my Texas constitution had not prepared me for this sort of weather. One very cold night that first winter after Jude was born, stuck in a house with an infant and a two-year-old, we lost power for a few hours. This cut off not only our light source but also our heat and water supply. We found ourselves planning for a night bundled up together in one bed with our young babies.

To give me some perspective, I thought of Laura Ingalls Wilder's autobiographical novel *The Long Winter*, when the Ingalls clan survives seven months of winter in a storehouse, eating nothing but potatoes and scant bread, keeping warm by twisting hay into fire fuel, nearly starving. I found myself wondering about the things Laura was perhaps too polite or optimistic to mention: How did they use the bathroom when they could barely survive getting out of bedclothes dusted with a layer of snow in the morning? Did they wash or change their clothes at all during that winter? How did they survive disease and malnourishment when their only source of food for many weeks was bread—bread made from grain that was hand-cranked into flour using a coffee grinder in shifts throughout the day?

Ours was a long winter for even the most seasoned of midwesterners. And when I saw signs of spring from our second-floor bedroom window where the little red buds on the maple tree bloomed first, I thought I had survived the worst and longest winter.

But harder winters were to come.

* * *

One late fall evening when Jude was three and Neva was five, Neva was bitten in the face by a dog. We were at the house of a friend who lived outside the community. When I saw Neva scoot away from the dog that she'd been trying to hug goodbye, her hand cupped against her face, mere centimeters from her eye, I wasn't sure what had really happened. Then the blood began dripping down her cheek, escaping the cradle of her hand. I lunged at her and pried her hand away. There was a deep wound in her cheek. I frantically scooped her up, and we drove to the hospital.

Neva recovered from the ten stitches and the trauma a lot quicker than I did. A week after she was bitten, I began to experience anxiety and panic attacks for the first time. The stress of community and farm tensions on my marriage and Neva's trauma had begun to exhume unarticulated fears, imaginings, and my own failings. Anxiety and depression sent me reeling into an even harsher winter than the winter of Jude's birth three years earlier. The weather was tough, but my interior landscape became a cold wilderness that seemed to blend into the white frozen horizon with no end. I don't exactly know how I kept my children fed and clothed that winter; I could hardly function. I couldn't eat, I lost weight, and there were moments while I was driving the bleak roads to town, as I watched the snow blowing across the crusty gray farm fields, that I imagined driving into an oncoming car just to escape the pain. I had never felt such inner desolation.

In the middle of February, my craving for the healing warmth of soil under my fingernails saw me starting my seeds inside the house too early. Flimsy black plastic trays lined the edges of my sliding glass doors. Their roots would be long enough to need more room before the soil in my garden was warm enough to transplant them. But I didn't care. If I could just see something grow, I could believe that spring was possible. I could believe that the tracks in the snow—ones that marked my anxiety-filled trips to feed the chickens—were melting into the dirt, providing the moisture it needed for another year of growth. I needed to see the snow melting and the sun rising.

And I did. And just as my fingers were aching to grow something tangible in the soil, life was taking root inside my body as well: I discovered I was pregnant with our third child. Even though this was unexpected, we were excited to tell the kids. We knew Neva and Jude would take to their older sibling duties with gusto.

My belly expanded into the warmth of those summer months in the sixth growing season, healing parts of me. But true healing isn't linear; it happens in fits and starts. Sometimes the tracks in the snow melt into the earth. And sometimes the snow covers them again and more are made.

Our lives had become waves of celebration and tension. Matthew and I realized that we could map out the farm seasons not by how well the farm had done or the health of the crops but by which major drama had occurred each year. The stress of five years in such an unsettled place began to catch up with both of us. Each winter, with the shorter days and so much more time to think, we wondered whether we should keep sticking it out for another farm season. It began to feel as though there were a fifth time of year: the season of dread.

In his book *Contemplative Prayer*, twentieth-century Cistercian monk and mystic Thomas Merton writes of the necessity of dread—dread leads you deeper. He says of a monk who is deep in monastic prayer:

> The Word of God which is his comfort is also his distress. The liturgy, which is his joy and which reveals to him the glory of God, cannot fill a heart that has not previously been humbled and emptied by dread. *Alleluia* is the song of the desert.[1]

> The monk who is truly a man of prayer and who seriously faces the challenge of his vocation in all its depth is by that very fact exposed to existential dread. . . . The monk confronts his own humanity and that of his world at the deepest and most central point where the void seems to open out into black despair.[2]

As I plunged more deeply into motherhood, I wondered what dread meant for a woman—one who, with her duties, couldn't be a monk in the practical ways of life. Maybe she was a mother and a wife, working in the naptime hours or caring for others, or maybe she was single and working outside the home. Maybe she had a loving husband who craved her body and emotional strength, or babies who needed her body to live, who needed her emotional strength to be healthy. She was tapped out, her needs forsaken not because her husband and children were at fault but because she idolized her marriage, she attached to the idea that motherhood was a calling. Instead of insisting on her need for the things that gave her life, she was afraid that her needs were the idols.

She needed to grow in her spirit. But sometimes it felt as though I didn't have the space to feel God's presence. The mystics seemed to dwell in places of constant search, marked by times of quietness and times of agony, periods that léad them into a deeper relationship with God. Many of them monastics and nuns, they all appear to live in extremities of solitude, silence, and prayer, where distractions are mostly internal.

Clearly they didn't have three young children. My solitude was extreme only in its absence.

Did I take a pass on mysticism when I became a mother and not a nun? Distractions abounded, and solitude took so much energy. And what was left for myself? What was left for God?

As I reached my mid-thirties, my hormones changing in normal ways, I was overcome by my own existential dread. Not from hours spent in solitary prayer—that was hardly ever a possibility—but from anxiety and depression. Were those anxious thoughts my prayers? Was this the kind of dread that should be my friend?

Maybe. Maybe dread was the only thing that made me desperate enough to ask God for help.

* * *

Mercifully, that sixth farm season was one of the first without a major drama. Matthew and the farm team had been working on the intern program, and it seemed their efforts had paid off. Along with two young interns on the farm, a young woman named Natalie, who had interned a few times before, moved to Plow Creek and became Matthew's first farm assistant. She was able to take on some jobs that made Matthew's workday shorter, and that meant he had more time for us.

That fall, with a birth even more swift and intense than Jude's, our third child, Annalee, was born. Neva was six and Jude was nearly four. They doted on Annalee and helped me face the coming winter months. I thought I had made it through the patches of anxiety, that my wilderness experience was finally over. I was naïve enough to think that the joy of having a newborn would override my emotional distress.

A few months after Annalee's birth, we met a young single mother who needed a place to stay. She had diabetes, her partner was in jail, and she didn't get along well with her mother, who'd been housing her. Her baby was just a few months older than Annalee. She obviously needed housing and help, and quickly.

She reached out to Plow Creek, hoping for a place to stay. When for various reasons Plow Creek couldn't accommodate her in communal housing, Matthew and I began to consider inviting her to stay with us. We had a guest room, and we'd been trying to find ways to show hospitality to people in our local community who might need aid. We went back and forth about the idea. I eventually said yes out of guilt, even though every other part of me was crying out against the decision.

The next week, I woke up in the middle of the night with a panic attack. It lit over my skin, singeing my whole body. It was as if I were an animal with bristles that must be burned off so that I could be devoured. The hardest part was that I knew the landscape of this frozen wilderness. I knew what was coming: the waking up before first light and remembering, catching the scent of the burning, knowing it was something I would have to carry through the day. My

mind churned through an illogical and imaginative reper-
toire of worries and fears.

The pain and anxiety I thought I'd conquered before I
got pregnant with Annalee was like a worm poking through
the skin of an apple it had made a path through. It had
been hidden inside the fruit and was still there, carving a
path for rot.

In a rare moment of quiet, I sat on a hill overlooking the
barns and the creek, chanting "Peace" into my heart, hoping for it to drench me, for God's light to pour upon my
dread. The tears came, but not the drenching peace, and I
was left with the darkness for another day.

And I felt ashamed.

18

Interlude:
Margery Kempe

MARGERY KEMPE isn't like the other mystics. Even though she is largely illiterate, she manages to dictate her entire autobiography, which becomes the first one of its kind in the English language. Unlike Francis, she isn't known for her saintlike, selfless deeds for others. Instead, her story is an angsty memoir of mental distress, of profound devotion to God, of a deepening separation from her husband, and of the agony and closeness to God that mystical visions bring.

A precursor to our millennial need to share the most exposing details of our lives, Margery's memoir is an awkward mess of emotional turmoil. I found it in equal measures refreshing and distressing.

She is born in 1373 in Norfolk, England, to an honorable father whose illustrious career includes terms as justice of the peace, a member of parliament, coroner, and mayor.

Not much is known about her childhood. She marries John Kempe, a man she eventually considers to be of lesser worth than her father.

Margery's autobiography begins with the "madness and spiritual crisis" that come as a result of the birth of the first of her fourteen children.[1] After a hard birth at the age of twenty, she begins to hear the voices of demons and spirits who tell her she will be damned if she doesn't confess. Mental anguish nearly overcomes her. She speaks of herself in the third person:

> And in this time she saw, as she thought, devils opening their mouths all alight with burning flames of fire, as if they would have swallowed her in, sometimes pawing at her. . . . She would have killed herself many a time as they stirred her to. . . . And also she pitilessly tore the skin on her body near her heart with her nails.[2]

When she tries to confess to a priest, for some reason he hastily rebukes her. She feels stopped up by the fear of her unspoken shame. That's when the demons enter into her visions in waves. Her frightened but loving husband is eventually forced to physically restrain her for many months while she tries to do as the demons bid her: kill herself.

And then suddenly, after months of terror, when she is alone for a few moments, a vision of Jesus appears before her, offering her his forgiveness and peace. Margery is so smitten by Christ that she vows to pursue him the rest of her life so that she might see a vision of him again. To do so she promises to forsake all others—including her husband.

She keeps that promise. Although she never joins a religious order, Margery preaches publicly, takes holy pilgrimages, weeps openly in the streets, and is arrested for heresy, though she is eventually released. In sum, she is a general source of bafflement for authorities and lay folk alike. She offends them because she dares to do what other women would not: speak about her experiences of God apart from the mediation or authority of any man.

19

Mother God

THE TRAIN rolled by in the distance and the wind was not a whisper but a roiling shout, whipping at my journal pages, rocking the hammock where I was trying to simultaneously write and keep Annalee asleep.

The cool weather felt like fall, but it was only August.

Fall weather continued to fill me with dread. Not because I didn't love fall, but because fall meant something else. It meant that winter was coming again soon.

I used to find winter charming, like a Texan loves Colorado because it is exotic and a little wild. Oh, those fluffy winter boots and fur-lined coats we only wear once a year on our ski trips. We were those sun-kissed vacationers who dabble in snowman-building before running inside to their rented cabins for some hot cocoa.

The previous two winters—one in which I was anxious after the dog bite, and one a bitter winter with an infant and two other young children—had left me breathless from anxiety and depression. I saw through the winter's charmed offering, and I was not tempted or amused. I no longer longed for the wild except in myself.

I was told God was wild, like Aslan, the lion of Narnia in C. S. Lewis's books: gentle but still full of a violent roar. Like Aslan, God wasn't safe, but he was good. Part of me loved that description of God.

But another part of me wanted a warm, motherly God.

I wonder if Margery Kempe felt the same need for a mother who would be both firm and nurturing in her love. Maybe this is why she sought approval from someone who saw God in the same way. Margery traveled to receive affirmation from another mystic, Julian of Norwich, in her cloistered cell. Julian wrote often of God, and particularly Christ, as both Mother and Father. Julian said of Jesus: "This fair lovely word Mother, it is so sweet and kind itself that it may not verily be said of none but him."[1]

In their meeting, Julian told Margery that she could feel confident in her mystical visions, her tears, and her encounters with God. But even though this meeting was transformative for Margery, it didn't allay her fears, and she spent many more years looking for validation for the odd manifestations of her spiritual devotion.

I too longed for counsel from a feminine God, one who would assure me that, yes, I was a mess. "But I knew that already, hon," she would say. "I made you. You're ashamed of your faults, but none of this is news to me."

Then she would say, in a Texas drawl not unlike my grandmother's, "Come on, darlin', stop your worry, now. Give up the shame. You're the one keepin' you from joy."

But just as Margery had trouble believing even Julian, these lessons of peace are often hard won.

* * *

The light on the ceiling of our bedroom was slanted in a parody of the open doorway, letting in the blue glow of

a nightlight from the hall. This nightly and usually innocuous shape hid something in the darkness; I could see
it creeping in the box made by the light that streamed in
through the half-open door, plotting something against
me, about to attack.

This wasn't anything new for me. Nightmares, night paralysis, and obsessive fears had been part of my life since I
was three years old, when my mom took me to a psycholo-
gist because I wouldn't leave her side, not even to go to the
bathroom at home.

When I was eight and still unwilling to let my mom
leave me alone in my room at bedtime, my mom, in an act
of desperation, performed a sort of exorcism on the closet
door that held the faces of dark monsters and demons in
the grains of wood.

In a junior high Bible class at our small Christian school,
we watched a video of a young man speaking from his jail
cell. It was one of those grainy, cautionary testimonials, although I'm not sure what they hoped to caution us against.
Asking Satan into our hearts, as this young man had done
with his friends? Murdering our parents in their sleep, as
they had done? Before this video, I'd never even considered
asking Satan into my heart. After the video, I couldn't stop
obsessing that I would do it accidentally.

I told my mom about these thoughts—thoughts I would
later learn are called obsessive or intrusive thoughts. At
the time, I was sure they were a sign that something was
irreparably wrong with me. But if my mom was worried
that I would murder her in her sleep, she didn't blink. She
sent me to the Psalms instead, and told me I was going to
be okay.

But still, those nighttime fears of demons, monsters,
and bad thoughts followed me off and on through my late
teens and into my twenties. Not only did they make me
afraid I was a terrible person, but they formed in my mind

a certain kind of likeness, more caricature than true por-
trait, of who God was. I began to take comfort in a less
mysterious Christianity. I went to grad school. I studied
theology. I became skeptical of great religious emotion. I
thought I could plaster away my sensitivities and obsessive thoughts behind a wall of intellectual belief. And it
worked for a while.

But my pretense of intellectual faith and skepticism of
religious experience didn't last.

In my thirties, with the challenges and bodily changes
of motherhood, the stresses of life in community, and the
onslaught of anxiety and depression, the plaster began to
crumble. Chunks of it now littered the floor. Something out
of my control began to climb out from behind the wall.

Franciscan friar and author Richard Rohr would say that
suffering and great love are catalysts for transformation.
Although I hesitate to say that I've suffered compared to so
many, I think what Rohr means is that the experiences that
break us apart are the ones which have the potential to really open us up to our true selves. If we latch onto them and
commit to spiritual practices, these experiences and disci-
plines can rewire our brains toward an openness to God.

This emotional distress blew my brain networks apart,
made me desperate. I began to feel like Margery Kempe:
afraid of the demons that erupted from the darkness of my
thoughts. I wondered if I was like her, and if the demons
that I'd tamped down with my logic and intellect were
creeping out to follow me.

For some mystics, like Catherine of Siena, the closeness
to the spiritual world was likely a sensitivity that developed
as a child. Catherine, a saint who lived in fourteenth-cen-
tury Italy, was six when she had her first vision of Christ.
Throughout her life she saw both the things of God and
unpleasant and terrifying voices and visions. Was I like
Margery Kempe and Catherine, born more sensitive to

the parting of the veil? Was that scared little child who didn't want to sleep alone really experiencing something supernatural?

When I began to experience those panic attacks after the birth of Annalee, I was ashamed. I told Matthew that I didn't think we would be able to host the single woman and her son, at least not when our baby was so young. I could hardly cope with my own life. How would I be able to open my home to a woman and her baby who needed extra care?

When Matthew told me that the woman had found a different situation, I was grateful. But still, the guilt swirled around the anxiety like a demonic dance. How could I be a good Christian and be unwilling to show hospitality to someone in need? I was torn between the need to push myself out of the relatively easy life I'd grown up with and the need for some comfort and peace. It was a gift to have grown up in such a way. But I didn't feel that I had entered into the suffering of others, looking for Jesus in the face of the single mother, the prisoner, the homeless. I felt ashamed that I couldn't make myself push through the pain to help someone else.

It took me a while to see that this tension was something I was going to have to lean into. My emotional winters were leading me to the mystics. The dark winter nights, and this fifth season of dread, were pushing me toward the Christ who came to Margery Kempe in her deepest distress.

20

Interlude:
Clare of Assisi

*I*N *HIS THIRTIETH YEAR*, Saint Francis's life is inter-
rupted by a young woman from a noble family. Whereas
Francis was a jovial merrymaker in his teen years, the pious
and passionate Clare already knows at age seventeen that
her family's wealth is a barrier. Wealth has separated her
from the poor who dwell outside the city walls, walls that
have protected her own rich family.

For a woman of her time, Clare is both headstrong
and meek. She never likes to be noticed, but even as her
parents begin to speak of her marriage prospects, Clare
hides a hair shirt under the lavish garments she's made
to wear.

When Clare falls in love with the way of Francis of
Assisi, it isn't a big surprise to the women of her household.
Clare's mother, Ortolana, made several pilgrimages to the
Holy Land, and has raised her daughters with such piety

and devotion to the church. It is Ortolana who first takes her daughters to hear Francis preach.

We can only imagine what Clare thinks and feels watching the quirky poor man, Francis, twelve years her senior, preaching during Lent. Clare, who by then is probably betrothed to some nobleman's son, finds her heart quickened by Francis's way of sharing the gospel: likely an exuberant but simple homily infused with all the passion, joy, and heartbreak he felt in his body. Clare is astonished by his words, and sends a message to Francis. Can she meet with him?

Clare meets her aunt Bianca in the quiet of a stone stairwell, in the secret hours of an Assisian night. So safeguarded are they by their holy, desperate prayers to bless this meeting that their skirts don't swish or crinkle as they steal out into the dark. Their prayers protect them from dangers as they trek out of the city gate and wade through a swamp to the Portiuncula chapel.

Francis and his companions are waiting for them. Clare gasps at the sight of the poor troubadour. Even though she has seen him many times, his ragged clothes seem to glow with holiness in the moonlight; he is beautiful and Clare is overcome. She falls at his knees, declaring her love for Christ and her commitment to follow his difficult way.

Francis is pleased by Clare. Francis, so ahead of his time, believes that the simple gospel he follows and preaches might eventually come up against the norms and boundaries of society. Bringing women into his community, one writer says, "appealed deeply to his imagination."[1]

Francis takes Clare by the shoulders and turns her around, guiding her to a chair in front of him. Fastening a cloth behind her neck so that her smock is protected, Francis himself shaves off her crowning glory, her long locks, tonsuring her like the other brothers. Then he and the friars usher her off to a Benedictine monastery for her protection.

A few days later, the men in Clare's family discover her absence. They saddle their horses and ride to find her. She is veiled when her uncle catches sight of her. Clare knows her uncle's violent tendencies; she has ministered to the bruises and cuts on the cheeks of her cousins and aunt.

Still, she comes out to meet him, the sunlight shining through the open doorway, illuminating the stones of the cloister. As he moves to grab her arm, raising his other hand to give her a beating, she pulls off her veil. Her uncle and his men step back, stunned into the silent, dark edges of the church, burned in their hearts by the light of her bare head.

Maybe they are changed by this burning in their hearts, by the witness of the brave girl who choses poverty and chastity over their wealth and excess. Or maybe they just know there is no way to salvage her reputation: no suitors will have her now.

After her family's failed attempt to force Clare to return home, it is only days later that her sister Catherine tries to follow in Clare's footsteps. The men of her family repeat their quest to take her back home, but this time, they drag Catherine down the hillside until she is nearly unconscious. Clare nurses her sister back to health, and when Catherine has recovered, she and the rest of their sisters join the Brothers of Francis. Eventually their following grows to include their mother, Ortolana, as well.

With her deep devotion to Francis and his strange ways of following the gospel, Clare will match him, albeit obediently, and she will continue to champion his cause even after his death.

21

The News

THE SUMMER after Annalee was born, with all three of my kids in tow, I met my mom and older sister, Heatherly, and some nieces and nephews at the Denver airport so we could fly to our next destination together. Although Matthew would surprise me by joining us a few days later, he was too busy on the farm to take a whole week off.

All of my side of the family lives in Texas, except for me. Our yearly gatherings, with my parents, my sisters, and their families, are usually jubilant and fun reunions. And every few years, we go back to a childhood vacation spot in Colorado. It's a place where we have some of our most vivid and joyful memories.

But this week was different.

At the airport, we performed the usual reunion rituals of hugs and decidedly southern, high-pitched cries of joy. With older nieces eager to watch my three young children, I took a quick airport date with Mom and Heatherly to get some coffee while we waited for our next flight.

As we stood in line, I asked when our father would be coming to the house in Colorado. I only got to see my dad on these occasional vacations to Colorado or Texas. I was used to his dropping in on our vacations at unexpected times. He loved a good surprise, but he also appreciated the freedom to come and go, to work and visit as he needed.

When my mom explained that he might not come, I was disappointed. My mom gave the slightest of glances to my sister.

"What's going on?" I said. Clearly Heatherly already knew something I didn't. My mom was silent for a moment, working up to something, trying to neatly unfold a deep emotion. I could tell she was endeavoring to preempt my own feelings with motherly comfort.

My dad's recent back trouble was getting worse, she said, and he was having some tests. Before she could explain what kind of tests, I knew what my mother was telling me. "You mean . . ."

"Yes," she said. "It could be cancer."

I didn't break down in sobs. I was surprisingly calm: it was a shock, but truthfully, I didn't really believe it. In my experience, health problems in my family were usually much milder than we first imagined, nothing that WebMD couldn't diagnose. In the past, my family's health issues had been the result of stress, or other issues that faded after a few days.

When we met up with my little sister, Elena, in our vacation house, she was especially weepy. She confided in me that she was scared. I soothed her but didn't understand why she was so upset. Surely a diagnosis of back strain would soon emerge, all those years of overseas travel ultimately taking their toll on my dad's seemingly immortal body.

It was July, and Annalee was eight months old. I'd been in counseling for my anxiety for a few months, and although it was helping, I didn't think that I could cope with anything else. As I listened to Elena's worries, I felt cut off from her emotions.

Dad surprised us by showing up midweek. After our brief hello, I walked in on him trying to pick up his luggage in his bedroom. He had stretched one foot all the way in front of him, and he was going to attempt to lift his bag with a straight leg despite the obvious pain he was in. When I rushed in to help, his smile of thanks was strained.

As I watched him over the next few days, the seriousness of his health issues became difficult to ignore. My father, normally vibrant and light on his feet, shuffled across the floor tiles all weekend, one hand constantly on his back. He grimaced when he thought no one was looking, and he changed the subject when anyone tried to ask him how he was doing.

In the middle of the week, my sisters, my mom, and I were sitting on a narrow stairway landing, speaking together in whispers and code. We hoped that the children, our dad, and our aging grandmother—who had dementia and didn't know anything about Dad's health—wouldn't hear. I was frustrated that our dad was so mute about what ailed him, that he kept everything close to the chest, and that he wouldn't share his emotions with us. The reasons for his silence weren't clear to us, and I could only speculate: he didn't trust feelings, he didn't want to burden us, he didn't want to accept his own emotions about things. Being the only one living away from the family was painful when all of this was happening. When I expressed this, Heatherly, who as the oldest child was bearing the brunt of responsibility for everyone's needs, pointed out that we needed to be compassionate and let our parents deal with things the way they knew how.

All my guilt about living far away while they all lived in the same town flared up, and I began to cry and lash out at her: Did she think I didn't know that? Just because I lived far away didn't mean I couldn't have an opinion. This was hard for me too!

When my mom stole quietly down the stairs in the middle of our argument, I felt humbled. It wasn't fair to fight in front of her. It wasn't fair to Heatherly that I reacted defensively. She and I had a good cry, we apologized, and we hugged. But the tension was high and so little of it was being expressed; we all sensed that we were just waiting for the inevitable.

At the end of the week of vacation, my dad called a meeting. In my dad's typical fashion, he only used the clinical scientific terms for the thing that was causing him pain in his back. The mass in his L2 vertebrae was adenocarcinoma. Translation: malignant growth. The C-word. Cancer. He would need radiation. Unfortunately, this kind of cancer doesn't originate in the spine. It had migrated from his esophagus, and it was an unusually aggressive cancer.

We sat around the room, Elena at my father's feet, asking gently probing questions that he didn't want to answer but did anyway. I went to bed in a daze. Matthew, the kids, and I left early the next morning to catch our flights back home. As we pulled up to the bustling chaos of Plow Creek after a long day of travel, I didn't feel peaceful.

I wasn't glad to be home. In fact, I didn't know what home was anymore.

22

Interlude:
The Cloister of the World

*C*LARE OF ASSISI lives in obedience to Francis, even calling herself his "little plant."[1] Modern minds might be turned off by the highly patristic language and behavior Clare uses. But she lives in a time where it is considered not only improper but dangerous for a woman to live without the protection of a man. And Clare does just that; she and her sisters, the Poor Ladies, live a Benedictine lifestyle in the convent of San Damiano.

Clare writes the Rule of Life for her companions and herself. After many years of struggle, she becomes the first woman to gain approval from Catholic Church authority for her Rule of Life, and she is able to live peacefully in her convent of women.

* * *

That week in Colorado, the rocking chair on the deck of the rental house became my solace. In between hikes in the mountains and family meals, I kept returning to the rocking chair on the porch with a book I'd been reading for a few weeks. I was taking one chapter at a time, not quite sure what it all meant, but I kept returning to it as a new spiritual practice.

I had begun reading Richard Rohr's *The Naked Now: Learning to See as the Mystics See* not to learn more about the mystics but to find a way to calm my swirling thoughts and anxieties, to learn to live in the moment instead of futurizing all my fears. But Rohr was introducing me to the mystics, about whom I knew very little. In his book, Rohr describes a lot about the mystics and their ways of seeing, and he suggests that all of us have access to seeing reality in a different way. Many mystics of the Christian tradition had a relationship with God that was beyond a purely intellectual view of faith. Francis's way blasted through the often complicated doctrines of the church to a simply lived gospel. He simply saw a different way, and he lived it.

Francis and Clare were both contemplatives, those who spend time with God in prayer and meditation. Though Clare was stuck behind the cloistered walls of a church, she always saw a different way, a way of finding God in the world. Francis, at many difficult moments, desired to hide away in a hermitage and spend all his time contemplating God. But some of his confidants encouraged him to look outward—to love God through loving the world, which requires being out *in* the world.

I wanted to know what was meant by contemplation. I wanted to see in this different way, to find a way to live in the present—as Rohr called it, "the naked now."

The mental distress that followed me into the daily tasks of my life was forcing me to seek help and look at my routines and habits of mind. In conversations with counselors, midwives, and friends, the idea of mindfulness kept coming up.

When I started practicing mindfulness—sitting quietly in a chair with my eyes closed, letting my thoughts drift away—I was looking for peace and calm. But I soon realized that I wanted a spiritual practice that was rooted in my Christian faith. I began to find solace and instruction with Catholic writers like Henri Nouwen, Richard Rohr, Thomas Merton, and these saints of old who lived contemplative lives of prayer.

In his book *Contemplative Prayer*, Merton suggests that contemplative prayer resists asking God for things or even looking for God. He writes that contemplative prayer is "a way of resting in him who we have found, who loves us, who is near to us, who comes to us to draw us to himself."[2]

But contemplative prayer was unsettling to me, especially in the beginning. Even though I knew better theologically, I was locked into a cycle of asking: of approaching God as a lucky charm, a wish granter who would give me what I longed for if I did everything I should. Instead, my prayer practice became an effort at not asking—of doing as Merton suggested and remaining in the presence of God, repeating a phrase, entering into prayer with the intention of being with God. It was a challenge, but I finally began to understand the "practice" part of spiritual practice: I had to rehearse over time so that the habit became ingrained in me throughout the rest of the day—when I did dishes, when I was speaking to my family, when someone annoyed me, and even when trauma or grief struck.

Every day for twenty minutes, I would sit in that rocking chair on the porch of our house in Colorado and quiet my thoughts, trusting God to take them and hold them for me.

I suppose I was looking for an escape from suffering and pain. But I quickly discovered that contemplation isn't for the faint of heart: after a while, I began to get nervous every time I sat down to pray.

The Catholic saints, the desert fathers, and mystics older than Saint Francis were known for contemplation and for intense and extreme devotion to the spiritual practices of prayer, meditation, and fasting. Saint Francis spent all of those days in a cave in the mountains near Assisi in contemplation and in mournful, penitent prayers of confession. Francis allowed himself to be spiritually stripped bare by God. He discovered in that cave a truer reality: that God comes to humanity, suffers with us, and calls us to love one another.

In her book *Franciscan Prayer*, Ilia Delio, a Franciscan sister, writes that both Saint Clare and Saint Francis viewed contemplation as a way of seeing and moving, of "seeing God in Christ with the eyes of the Spirit" in order to move toward a "vision of God's humility . . . God's humbling movement toward humanity."[3] But Delio says that it was Clare who made clearer the path of Franciscan prayer. Franciscans were known to be prayerful, but they didn't have any clear writings from Francis on how to pray. Clare, who lived under the strict Benedictine rule of life, longed to combine the marks of monasticism—contemplation, spiritual union with God, and transcendence—with what Delio calls the "evangelical life," which is focused outside the cloistered walls on loving God through the love of others. The monastic and cloistered life Clare was leading focused on solitude and silence. But Clare longed for an evangelical, outward approach to life, one that was focused on imitating Christ in the "cloister of the world."[4]

For Clare, contemplation of God, and particularly of Jesus on the cross, meant a deeper awareness of God's presence in humanity and therefore a deeper awareness of her own suffering.

As I began to practice contemplation, I realized that I didn't need a discipline that helped me avoid the suffering in the world. Instead, I needed a practice to help me enter more deeply into the suffering of others. I began to be nervous when I sat down to pray because I realized that contemplative prayer was not about simply finding peace. In fact, it was leading me deeper into the pain of the world. Contemplative prayer was unsettling me so that God could show me true reality.

Surely, this wouldn't have been surprising to Clare. She knew that our union with God was not the only goal of these prayers. Delio says, "Whereas the monastic path ends at contemplation, for Clare, the goal of prayer is imitation." Our prayers lead us to love God's creation and creatures more, and ultimately, "we become what we love."[5]

I desperately wanted to become more like the God who loved. But how was I to get there? Would prayer be enough?

23

Letter to Margery Kempe: Get Thee to a Mental Health Professional

Dear Margery,

When I started reading your memoir after the birth of my third child, I felt a kinship, a mother-to-mother connection. Sometimes I just wanted to embrace you and run a soothing hand over your sweaty brow. I agonized with you in your mental distress; I think I had sensitivities to the spiritual world when I was younger, ones that I tried to brick away behind an intellectual wall.

But I also think you could have used a more sensitive midwife and a few strong prescriptions to counteract your postpartum depression. As someone who struggled with postpartum depression, I'm not making light of your agonies, but I suspect you might have been diagnosed pretty quickly. I imagine that birthing fourteen children messes with your hormones. Perhaps with a bit of counseling and medication, you and your husband could have been a lot more joyful in marriage and parenthood.

Maybe I have you all wrong, Margery. Maybe I should take you at face value, believing that you really had visions of both Jesus and demons. If that's the case, then your agony and angst is more than I can handle. When I begin to believe your visions, the demons you saw seem to reach into my dreams, telling me I can't escape them. I begin to feel distressed reading your words, as if my old anxiety is tugging at me, looking for a foothold.

Maybe you did really have a special mystical connection to Jesus that I've never had. I envy you on that point: your vision of Jesus was so real and fulfilling that you spent the rest of your life searching for him. Did your open connection to the grace of the spiritual world also leave you exposed to the flood of less savory powers?

Please don't take this the wrong way, but sometimes it seems that you milked your agonies a little. And when I say "milked," I'm not referring to the fact that an anchorite told you that you were nursing at Jesus' breast. I mean, I have happily breastfed my babies, but I think we can all agree that a good editor would have done away with that mental image for all of history. But you did wander the streets weeping profusely. Perhaps I'm judging you and perhaps you couldn't help it. Maybe Julian of Norwich was right that they truly were a gift from God: your agony and distress.

As someone who has suffered a small fraction of what you have, I offer you my compassion, but I cannot follow you any further. In conclusion, Margery, I bid you adieu and leave you in the hands of men and women less susceptible to imagining that they could lose their sanity.

Your friend (who is, frankly, trying to avoid seeing any more demons on her bedroom wall),

Christiana

24

Letter to Clare of Assisi:
Mother of God

Dear Clare,

I hope you don't mind if I disturb you. I've already pressed so many words on your companion, Francis, who is teaching me about simplicity. But it seems that you are the expert on solitude and prayer. I doubt that you would take that honor for yourself. But I know that whenever you were troubled, you would contemplate the crucified Christ, closing your eyes and imagining yourself kneeling before his body, blood dripping from his wounds.

This is a strange image for my culture. We may have progressed in some areas during the centuries since you lived (I'm not ready to give up stoves, toilets, and hot showers). But in our efforts to be unique individuals, we have lost the gifts of communal life, communal habits, and customs. We tend to skip the lament, to brush past the grief. In that loss,

we have also given up the agony of Jesus' death. We want
to get to the resurrection, to the image of the risen Christ. It
makes sense that a culture that prizes the comfort and cleanliness of toilets over throwing waste in the streets would shy
away from anything too messy.

Just like Francis, you gave up your wealth in order to embrace
the mess of life. We are foolish if we think that avoiding the
mess will bring us peace or bring us closer to God. You and
Francis knew that well, both in life and in death.

I decided to contemplate the crucified Jesus, just as you did,
Clare. On a bleak day, when it was so easy to despair at the
news from our world, I sat in my study room at the library,
closed my eyes, and focused on Christ on the cross. I saw him
bleeding; I heard him groan and struggle to breathe.

But then I saw *her*. At the foot of the cross she lay, her arms
draped around the splintered wood, cradling it softly so as
not to shake the cross and cause her son more pain.

Of all the people in Jesus' life, his mother, Mary, suffered
most acutely. Mary, only a decade or so older than I am now,
watches the suffering of her son. She smells his blood, longs
to dry his sweat and take his place. Maybe she thinks of the
day the angel came to her and wonders how it could end this
way.

She was raised in a home where the sound of her elders—
their voices gnarled like fig trees—and the rhythm of feet
learning balance on stone floors mixed together in a song of
home. But suddenly, with the beating of angel's wings, this
girl, this vessel of the long-expected, began to grow a secret.
As cells multiplied and burrowed deep into soft lining, as
brain and heart formed a one-and-only God-man inside her,
this girl Mary feared disgrace.

When the prophet Isaiah called the Messiah "Immanuel," a name that means "God with us," he was singing a song of comfort for the poor, the pained, those suffering from war and violence. But when was God truly first with us? Was it in the cries that struck at the animals' ears as Baby Jesus was born in their stable? Was it when the scent of soap rose from the holy earthly skin before it was touched by a world that would tear his flesh?

No. God was not with us first, but with her: the lonely young virgin who held a secret Spirit instead of a lover. She knew the Son of Man first as intimately as blood.

Jesus' blood might have been holy, but it was Mary's blood, too, that poured out of his flesh, dripping down the wood of the cross he'd carried through the streets. Clare, I wonder: Were the wounds of your beloved Francis—stigmata wounds that burst forth from his hands and feet—were they oozing with his own blood? Or was it the blood of Jesus? Was it the blood of Mary too?

Mary knew what it was like to be wounded. She knew true poverty more than the rest of us. Perhaps it is Mary's blood in every stigmata wound.

As I think of Mary and of the babies I have birthed, I think of the stigmata. I think of blood. I think of womanhood, motherhood, and the woundedness that being a parent requires. When Francis had to learn to love the leper the way a parent loves her child, maybe his stigmata were not only a way to feel the wounds of Christ but a way to feel the wounds that you would understand: the wounds of womanhood.

Every birth is full of blood, pain, and water, flowing from a place that was home to a child. When that home breaks open, both mother and child are wounded by it. A mother contends with the cramps, scars, tears, biting, and tugging. The child must learn to live in the coldness, hunger, and blinding brightness of life.

It is like this with every mother, whether she has birthed her baby or not. Every day she is wounded even more: by tantrums, lack of sleep, feedings, screams, giggles, and deep love. A mother learns to love her baby more as she cares for her child, but every moment of care leaves her more raw and wounded. Nothing will hurt more than if her baby is taken away.

Mary is intruded upon by God, deeply wounded by the Holy Spirit, brought into the deepest poverty by the preposterous words of an angel. When her baby is taken from her, when he bears the weight of his own body and blood, she is broken apart.

What a sorrow, what a stigmata it is to love a child! But just as Jesus had Mary's blood in his veins, perhaps we all have the blood of Jesus in ours. The blood that wounds and heals, that bursts out of Saint Francis from longing and oneness. By Christ's blood we are healed, we are unified, we are wounded. We cannot love without wounds.

When you contemplated the crucified Christ, Clare, did you see that the God who was rich in everything came down and gave it all away? In your letters to Agnes of Prague, you abstained from explaining the cross. Instead, you drew Agnes to the conclusion that "the crucified Christ reveals to us the God of love who has taken on our humanity, lived in poverty and died on a cross. He is our path to life . . . because heaven is an unimaginable relationship with God in love."[1] Paradoxically, "the poverty of God is the true source of our riches."[2] Clare, I think you saw that in contemplating Christ in this way, you were moved to poverty, a poverty that made you rich in God. In this relationship and contemplation, you became what you loved and longed for, and therefore your love spilled out to others.

When I contemplated the crucified Christ that day in the library, I saw that Mary's woundedness was my own.

This makes perfect sense, really. Or maybe it only makes sense in the way that God's foolishness is wiser than my wisdom. Brother Lawrence, a mystic who lived many years after you did, in seventeenth-century France, finally knew this truth on a regular day in the middle of winter: "Gazing at a barren tree in winter, Lawrence saw for the first time the majesty of God's grace and the constancy of God's providence. He imagined himself like a tree, waiting for the life that God would inevitably bring in season."[3]

After this revelation, Lawrence went to live at a monastery in Paris and spent his life finding God in the minutiae of his daily work as a lay brother.[4] Lawrence knew the same truth that you did, Clare, even as a young girl from a wealthy family: that our strength comes not in our wealth, beauty, power, or even good mental health. Our strength comes when we are barren, naked, suffering, and sad. Or when we are willing to look upon and lean into the suffering of others. For when we do that, we are truly seeing Christ on the cross.

Thank you for teaching me this.

Your humble servant,

Christiana

PART IV

CHURCH

The Church is the cross on which Christ was crucified;
one could not separate Christ from His Cross,
and one must live in a state of permanent
dissatisfaction with the Church.

—Dorothy Day quoting Romano Guardini, *The*
Long Loneliness

25

A New Kind of Family

AFTER SOME PAINFUL YEARS in community, when things looked as though they might fade and decay, our meetings of processing and restructuring seemed to suddenly bear fruit. In addition to Angela and Matt's two newly adopted children in our midst, Plow Creek was joined by a new family, a newly married couple named Natalie and Allan, and two single people. A system for welcoming new members was put in place, our worship times felt fuller, and God seemed to be answering our prayers for new life.

One of these new members, Dave Bell, entered our life with a tuneful laugh. Although he was often in pain from a degenerative disease and his rheumatoid arthritis made his limbs swell, he was always smiling, always joking, and never complaining. His surname was highly appropriate, as Dave necessitated a sparkling cliché; he truly had a twinkle in his eye.

A fiftysomething (he didn't like to tell his age) bachelor farmer who had lived in the area most of his life,

Dave owned a farm at the base of a deep plunge in the road named Pig Farm Road. It was named for Dave's farm, where the previous owner used to raise pigs before he bought it. It turned out we could see his farm from the west side of the Plow Creek property, at a spot called Daisy Hill; if you followed our creek all the way to its end, there was Dave's house.

It seems Dave was meant to be among us.

Matthew, who'd joined the local volunteer fire department, had met Dave one day at the party of another farmer.

"You see that guy over there?" said a friend to Dave. He pointed to Matthew.

"Yeah."

"You'd like him. He's smart. And he talks about interesting things."

Dave approached Matthew, and an unlikely friendship between two farmers of differing ages and backgrounds—a friendship largely based on their mutual love of self-deprecating humor—was born.

* * *

Dave began to help out around the farm, too, offering Matthew much-needed advice on how to raise pigs. When our first expectant sows were ready to give birth, Dave spent most of his free hours inside the dusty makeshift birthing center he and Matthew had built together, protecting the jumpy mother pigs from curious community visitors who would have loved to see the birth of piglets.

When Matthew needed help with hay, tilling, or harvesting because he didn't have the right machinery, Dave connected him with local farmers who offered their services. He told us stories of the way farmers used to progress from one farm to the next during harvest season, helping one another out. Farming in these areas was not about competition but community.

One evening during the growing season, we had an impromptu backyard dinner party on the picnic tables we shared with our neighbors Matt and Angela. Dave came driving up in his red pickup truck to check on the pigs in the back barn. We called him over to join us. He rubbed his hands together in the mischievous way a boy might do just before he annoyed his sister. Dave was being invited to do three of the things he loved most: eat with others, tease his friends, and drink cheap beer.

As our children began to explore the woods behind the house, their screams and chants lifting into the air with the last light, the conversation between the adults turned mystical. Maybe it was the magic of the fireflies as they sparked the summer evening with an otherworldly light. Maybe it was the red wine, loosening our tongues into revealing our truths and fears. Or maybe it was just time for a revelation.

I made an offhand comment about the visions I saw in my room at night. It started with the Native American chief who appeared at the foot of my bed a year after we moved to Plow Creek. When I learned later that the surrounding area used to be one of the largest settlements of Potawatomi, I wondered if he'd been a ghost, telling me something about what our ancestors had done to his people, about the land I lived on that he'd been forced to relinquish. The visions had become more frequent in the last few years: I saw a deranged rabbit, a monster, creepy children. I was always left with the feeling that the creatures in the room were plotting against me, trying to trick me into believing I was imagining things. Was it some leftover spiritual pain from the previous tenants, was it a mystical connection, or was it just my own anxiety about life? Or could those all be a part of the same whole?

With each of my descriptions, our neighbor Matt slowly leaned back on the bench. "Whoa, you're freaking me out a little," he said to me.

"It could all be just a product of my mind," I said, trying to laugh off his intensity. But I had to admit, it often made me uneasy too.

"We went over our house with burning sage and prayers before we moved in," Angela said. She was no stranger to inexplicable things that might or might not be of the spiritual realm. She had grown up in charismatic congregations and had stories to tell about people anointing her, prophesying over her, and getting clear visions. After years away from it, she couldn't deny the realities of her experience, but she wondered if these things were hyped up or true.

Dave, who'd grown up in the area, began to tell us about the one trip he took with a mission group to Canada. Apparently he drove his group leader to distraction with his antics. But it was the encounters with various church leaders on the trip that shook him up. In one congregation the group visited, Dave began to see a malevolent creature at the doorway. Not long after, two leaders of different congregations independently claimed that they could see that Dave had some kind of monster hovering around him. They prayed the creature away from him.

I'd heard Dave tell stories of his visions before, one being a palpable and visible sense of the Holy Spirit at a time when he wasn't at all interested in God or the church. But as we sat outside that summer evening, our colors and temperatures raised by the thrill of the conversation and the night, it hit me.

"Dave! You're a mystic," I shouted.

"What do you mean by that?" Dave snorted, a giggle in his throat.

"You've had visions of God, and you've also had visions of strange creatures. Maybe you have this throughline to God that most of us don't have."

"Well," he demurred, as was characteristic whenever a potential compliment was on the horizon. "I don't know about that."

But I was convinced, not only because of his visions but because of what I found a lot more interesting: his works of mercy. For many years before it finally closed, Dave worked as the house parent for a children's home in the area, one that took in young men from abusive and violent situations.

I suddenly understood: Dave was a mystic *and* a misfit.

The next morning as I glanced out of Annalee's bedroom window, I saw a sight that didn't surprise me but pleased me immensely. Our neighbor Matt was circling the edges of our house, waving a smoking clump of sage in the air, saying prayers to bless and guard our house.

* * *

Because of the new membership at Plow Creek, after Annalee was born I rarely needed to ask for help with childcare on Sunday mornings at church. Even though I was on the music team every Sunday and led worship with Matthew once a month, I knew I had no reason to call anyone ahead of time to ask for help. I just showed up, baby in tow, and handed the baby over to Dave.

Dave spent many worship services carrying Annalee back and forth across the linoleum floor while I played the guitar and Matthew preached. When Dave wasn't available, Natalie, Allan, or Angela were on hand to help.

As my youngest daughter began to talk, Annalee and Dave formed a bond. When our dog began pacing the living room floor, whining to get out, we knew that Dave had driven up in his red pickup truck and that Ginger, Dave's golden retriever, was outside waiting to play. Annalee would toddle over to the screen door and cry, "Dave! Dave!"

"Hi, little skeezy," he would say, poking a finger at her through the hole in our screen door.

And when he'd come over for dinner or small group, Annalee's declaration that "Dave's a rascal" would leave him in stitches. Annalee had clearly adopted Dave into our family. And he wasn't interested in going anywhere either.

* * *

Newcomers like Dave helped expand the way Matthew and I viewed our marriage and our family life. It took me several years of marriage and community to remember the way I had felt as a single woman: that the culture of our Christian churches frequently sees the goal of the Christian life culminating with marriage and family. And those outside these traditional families are often left to fend for themselves on the edges of the church. Looking out onto the vast sea of church programs for families, parents, and married couples was disheartening to me before I married Matthew. It seemed that family values were prized above most anything else and that what I had to offer wasn't as treasured until I was married with kids.

Although he preached on the ills of divorce, Jesus had some uncomfortable things to say about families. There are several biblical passages in which Jesus challenges the traditional family narrative of his day. In his book *Oriented to Faith*, Tim Otto points out that it is "startling . . . how often Jesus speaks against and disrupts family."[1]

Even as a boy—when his parents search for him for days, only to discover that he has been at the temple, amazing the chief priests and teachers—Jesus has a sense that God's parenthood is more important than his earthly family. Early in his ministry, Jesus pulls his new disciples away from the fishing business their fathers have passed down to them. He tells a "would-be disciple who wants to bury his father to 'let the dead bury their own dead.'"[2] In Matthew, when someone interrupts Jesus' teaching to tell him that his family of origin has arrived and they'd like to speak with him, instead of acknowledging them, Jesus points to his disciples and claims them as family, saying, "Here are my mother and my brothers. For whoever does the will of my Father in heaven is my brother and sister and mother" (Matthew 12:49-50). These words are hard to hear for faith communities that prize the family above all other loyalties. But Jesus is expanding our view of who our family is.[3]

Later in the New Testament, Paul encourages the new believers to see their brothers and sisters in Christ as their primary family. As a single gay man, Tim Otto felt desperately alone and on the outside of the church's closed-off family units. But when he began to study what Jesus and the New Testament writers said about family, Otto took courage in this idea of family being beyond blood ties. And later he joined one of Plow Creek's sister intentional communities, where he found a place among a wide array of people who supported and encouraged him and became his family.

In its very structure, Plow Creek had something unique to offer those who didn't fit the traditional family mold: it encouraged the voices of those who were single or didn't have children. And the structure of the church and community meetings was adopted to avoid privileging one voice over another. Not only were those less apt to speak up encouraged to voice an opinion, but those who were single or without children were given equal opportunity to be in leadership positions, whether that meant being on the leadership team or facilitating worship.

Plow Creek adopted its leadership structures from the way Jesus lead and served, and the things he taught about how we should view our biological bonds. And our deeper relationships with our brothers and sisters in community showed Matthew and me that our family unit could offer something to those beyond our biological family. We could become family with others.

26

Interlude:
What Does the Lord Require?

*F*RANCIS IS DESPERATE for a break. He is tired, struggling with ill health, and can't keep up with caring for and about all his followers. He is the overwhelmed, oversaturated, and overstimulated leader of a crew of motley misfit brothers (and, peripherally, sisters). Frankly, he is beginning to long for the life of the hermits, whose hours are occupied in solitary prayer under the stars, in caves, or even, if they want, holes dug in the ground. The point is, they are free to pursue God without distractions, responsibilities, or other people. Isn't it about time for Francis to finally release himself into the contemplative silence of perfect union with God?

It's a good thing that Francis has bound himself to the rule of life he'd created—a rule that commands he consult two trusted confidants for their discernment before he makes any momentous decision.[1]

Who are his confidants? Sylvester, one of his first followers, and Clare, a friend who has become essential and beloved to him. He sends his messenger, Masseo, to beg them to offer prayers on his behalf, to help him discern if he "should preach or devote myself entirely to prayer."[2]

Sylvester's answer reaches Masseo quickly. Clare's answer, although later in coming, is the same.

When Masseo comes to Francis with their answers, before the future saint asks him to relay the information, he gives his messenger food and washes his feet. Then he humbles himself again before Masseo and, trembling, asks him for the answer.

"What does the Lord require of me, Masseo?"

Masseo's answer is hard for Francis to hear. "He wants you to preach wherever you are, for God did not bring you this far for yourself alone, but for the saving of many others."[3]

Francis's wish to be a hermit who cloisters himself in isolation is denied. Instead, Francis is called back to his life in the cloister of the world, reaching out to others. And, in true Francis fashion, he leaps toward his continued life as a friar with renewed enthusiasm and obedience.

* * *

Clare and Francis both knew that their conversion meant something significant, even with regard to their biological family. Although there was a violent fracturing of Clare's family in terms of her male relatives, her mother and sisters became a new spiritual family, held together by a bond even greater than blood.

Francis's break from his family was as dramatic and bordering on violence as it might have needed to be for a young man in his culture and time who was expected to take on the vocation of his father. Then, just as he desires to break from his chosen family later in life, just when he believes he needs to seek a life of solitude, it is the words of his wise friends that return him to the fold of family. This time, however, it is a family defined not by biology but by the bonds of Christ.

27

Blowing Your Nose in Church

*W*HEN I WAS in college, I had three roommates from tiny towns in Texas. They were hilarious, and they managed to laugh at me while making me feel absolutely wonderful because of it. Those women laughed at me because they saw something absurd and quirky in me. Instead of feeling mocked, I felt known and adored.

It was the way Jesus might have laughed at Peter when he asked a passionately stupid question, or the way he pulled Thomas in to poke at his wounds. The way he shook his head at the quaking disciples on the boat during the storm; perhaps they missed the smirk he hid behind his hand.

Jesus adored them and knew them.

One of these roommates, Ann, had a way of collecting people the way Jesus did. She had a way of launching her heart out wide and pulling the lonely, the hurt, the friendless back in with it.

I don't know exactly where Ann met her, but a young woman named Peggy suddenly started to hang around our college house. Before I knew it, Peggy started coming to church with us on Sundays. Peggy was a rather unpleasant person; she had few social skills to speak of, she was always groaning about something, and she blew her nose like a cartoon character. It was like a horn honking and puffing in the middle of the quietest moments in church.

Introvert that I was, I sometimes dreaded those mornings of getting ready for church, when Ann would stand at my bedroom door and call my name in her mirthful, sing-songy way. "Christiana? Christiana?"

"Yes?" I'd groan.

"Can we pick up Peggy on the way to church?"

I wanted to get to church without a fuss, to remain as withdrawn as I could, to be with the people I knew, and to get to lunch afterward. Any inconvenient interruptions on the road to church would ruffle my comfortable expectations. Still, I couldn't resist Ann's laughing insistence, so we'd drive from our house off campus and pick up Peggy in front of her dorm. She would make us wait, unapologetically, then shuffle out of the lobby and into the car, and without pleasantries or thank yous, she'd accept our ride to church.

And in the middle of the sermon, the tissue would come out of the pocket and the honking would begin. I'd groan each time, but I couldn't say no to Ann. I knew that Ann's heart was bigger. I knew that she was the good Samaritan and was forcing me to watch as she tugged the hurt girl onto her horse and carried her to care.

I knew that her heart was more open than mine. But I didn't know yet how to follow her example.

***

There was literally no bread to break as we gathered together in the Plow Creek common building. The serving table, stained with the juices and sauces of potlucks past, was full of pasta. Five pasta dishes, to be exact. We were all sagging from the weight of the farm season, our jobs, and nurturing our children, and pasta, at least, was simple.

So we sang a song of grace—quite possibly "For the Beauty of the Earth," "Johnny Appleseed," or the doxology—and grabbed the white plastic plates from their stack. They were etched with knife cuts, witnessing to their thirty (or more) years of use and repeated washings in the common building's sink by helpers chosen from a rotating list every week. (We'd all try to avoid eye contact with whomever assigned the dishwashers on a particular night—except for Meg, whose servant heart urged her to clean even when it wasn't her turn.)

We helped our children pile their dishes with vegetable pasta, mac and cheese, or spaghetti meat sauce, knowing that whatever was heaped on would be scraped off into the compost, half eaten, in a few minutes when they ran outside to play. And we sat and ate together.

Conversation could be easy. We had history together. We spent the week sharing prayer requests, joys, and the mundane tasks of daily life, like farm work or childcare swaps or Saturday projects.

But it could also be awkward. Our vulnerability with each other could bleed into a melancholy that we passed back and forth. In these moments, I felt a kinship with the early church: their quarrels and broken relationships. Sometimes I imagined the apostle Paul rebuking our nitpicking, our tendency to see the worst in each other. I saw Jesus pointing at me, saying, "Is it so hard to be kind when I have given you so much kindness?"

Living in intentional Christian community is like being a part of a family, one that you choose, but then you can't decide whether you want to keep choosing them, because they keep bringing up the same issues that trigger your anger or frustration. You realize, after years together, that each of you has scratches, certain points in your album that keep skipping and repeating the same needs, the same hurts, the same prayers.

It's funny the way God breaks your heart open: through children who won't stop demanding love, attention, and nurture; through awkward conversations with neighbors who say the wrong things and who interrupt; through people who make you remember the feeling of being with Peggy, blowing her nose loudly during a church service.

After years in community, believing myself to be fairly "normal," my anxiety extended to social situations. One trip to a writing festival nearly sent me into full panic attack mode. I felt awkward, weird, and unacceptable. I said strange things when I was nervous and just stared with a big, dopey smile at people I'd just met.

I wonder if grief played a part in my feeling of awkwardness too. How can you make small talk and paste on a smile when your father is suffering from cancer?

Then something occurred to me: perhaps it's my privilege that led me to believe that God used others to open my heart, as if they were pawns in a game meant to lead me down the perfect life path, to learn the perfect and most beautiful truths. Perhaps God was teaching *me* that I was a lot like Peggy too: lost, lonely, and awkward, grieving, blowing my nose too loudly at the most sacred moments.

Maybe that's the way Saint Francis and some of the other mystics felt too: that what held them back were the things that repulsed them. Embracing pain, suffering, and yes, even awkwardness, were the first steps in understanding the suffering of others.

28

Interlude:
Awkward Anarchist

*S*IMONE WEIL—philosopher, pacifist, anarchist, radical, unchurched believer, unintentional mystic—is dowdy and awkward. She wears round spectacles. Her hair is a frizzy bob. She wears the baggy, colorless attire of a factory worker, and her unsmiling mouth is so pronounced that it's clear she has an overbite.

Simone means to portray herself this way. Earlier in her life she was considered quite beautiful, but Simone has become fierce in her intent to obliterate that which is outwardly lovely and "superficially charming" in herself. Her photographs capture a woman whose likeness is "absolute in its refusal to be charming, an exaggeration, almost a caricature." Father Perrin, a close friend and confidant of Simone's, describes her clothes as a "costume" she wears that is intentionally awkward and makes her appear "clumsy" and "shapeless."[1]

The facts of Simone Weil's life are scant, but the impact of her writings is immeasurable. She is born in the early part of the twentieth century, a decade after Dorothy Day, in Paris, France. Though her heritage is Jewish, her parents are agnostic, and she is taught that religion is legalistic and oppressive.

Still, despite this lack of religious education, from a very early age, Simone has odd tendencies and behaviors that are reminiscent of other mystics. She has an early compassion for the suffering of others that is so pronounced that even as a five-year-old, she "refused to eat sugar, as long as the soldiers at the front were not able to get it."[2] Simone's actions, born of compassion and perhaps the guilt of her privilege, only get more extreme with age. Some even say she is "absurd" in the great lengths she takes to empathize with the poor and oppressed.[3]

Simone and her older brother are intellectual prodigies, and when she graduates from university, her teacher calls her a "philosophical genius." But she will need to be careful not to speak and write with such heady language, he says, which makes it difficult for her to communicate to others. After graduation, she teaches philosophy for a short while before taking a year off to do physical labor in the fields in order to "experience fully the working people's life."[4] This is a theme of her life: study and teaching, taking breaks to live the life of a laborer—and all the while her health suffers.

Reminiscent of Saint Francis and many of the mystics, Simone adopts a routine of self-abnegation bordering on the ridiculous. She keeps herself from physical affection, avoids love interests, and adopts a masculine appearance. Even though her health is often fragile, she gives up teaching to live the hard life of a factory worker.

In her early thirties, Simone meets Father Perrin, a Dominican priest who will have a great influence on her spiritual life. Eventually, the letters the two write one another will be among her most famous writings.

In 1943, already in ill health, Simone travels to London for a research job. Though doctors urge her to keep up her nourishment, she refuses to rest or eat more than the rations that those in German-occupied zones in France are allowed during the war. She is diagnosed with tuberculosis and hospitalized. At the age of thirty-four, she dies.

29

Worship

*E*VERYTHING about the church was foreign.

Thirty minutes earlier, I'd climbed the stone steps to the second floor, steps that—given the location of the church, the look of the buildings around it, and the smooth depressions in the stone—were likely hundreds of years old. It was my first attempt at finding a church in the small village in Scotland where I'd moved only weeks earlier for grad school, knowing no one.

Although years of greeting guests at my home church and travel overseas had trained me to fake it, I was generally nervous about meeting new people. And this was too much for me.

When the worship service started, I didn't know what to do. It was a low-church gathering like the Church of Christ services I'd grown up with, but the inclusion of boisterous instruments was jarring for a girl from an acapella tradition. However, I think it was the streamers that undid me. Growing up in a tradition that leaned toward intellectual faith rather than expressed emotion, I was unable to cope with the streamers waving around the congregation during a praise song. And when the tambourines came out and a mother put bells on her baby's socks, I couldn't take it anymore. My face warm with embarrassment, I quickly walked out in the middle of the service.

I'm not sure if I was offended, embarrassed, or frightened by the charismatic display of worship. But it unnerved me so much that I found a solemn, liturgical Episcopal church filled with proper British people and joined the choir for the next four years of Sundays.

* * *

When we entered worship at Plow Creek to find the chairs arranged differently, I was unfazed. I'd started to become accustomed to the ways Sunday worship services at Plow Creek were conducted: at times creatively and at times haphazardly. One Sunday, the guitar player who happened to be facilitating worship told us he had come up with his meditation while sitting in his deer stand the night before.

But today we had another worship leader, and this one had chosen dancing as the theme. So he had pushed all the chairs against the walls in preparation for a dance-filled worship service that included leaping and other forms of interpretive dance.

I sat against the wall, my head leaned back and eyes closed. I'm sure it looked like I was being very spiritual. And believe me, I was trying to be open-minded and worshipful. But really, what took the greatest effort was avoiding the sight of those who'd chosen to dance, bounding across the room, most earnestly, in time to the music.

* * *

The scent of Louise's baking—caramel pecan, apricot cinnamon, and butterhorn rolls—hung about as I pushed open the heavy door of the common building. On bakery days during the summer, I could expect these smells when I dashed in to collect my community mail or food from the co-op room downstairs. But today was a special worship service. I was hungry, breathless from the walk up the hill from our house in the valley.

Normally, I would be here early on Sundays, practicing with the music team. I'd been leading worship for a few years now. I'd loved playing guitar, but I was limited and self-taught and nervous even in front of our small group of worshipers. Then one day, Mark asked me to join the music team; gradually, I became a worship leader, relying on my remedial ability to play the guitar, my singing, and my emerging love for choosing and teaching new music.

Today, I was relieved to be free from doing music for once and eager to see what this service would look like. A few weeks after Easter, we traditionally celebrated Jesus' appearance to his disciples after his resurrection. Early on that Sunday morning, we would gather in the common building for a fish breakfast. We'd eat baked fish (or fried fish sticks) and Louise's rolls, drink coffee or juice, and commemorate together that early morning meal when the risen Christ startled his disciples on the beach.

But this year's fish breakfast was a little different. For the first time in six years, new members had joined our small church. After the membership ceremony, the real initiation into community life began. It was then that they were confronted with two straightforward and inescapable questions, presented by a committee member drowning in work: "Where can you serve?" and "When can you cook your first Sunday lunch?"

When the new folks showed understandable hesitation about cooking for thirty people, I assured them: "I couldn't cook when I moved here seven years ago, but now I cook a large meal without blinking." (As long as someone helps with dishes, that is.)

Their first major task was to plan the fish breakfast. There was a strange push and pull when a task was handed over to someone new. After seven years, Matthew and I were now a part of the middle generation of this community. We still remembered the idealistic excitement of being new members, but we also understood that the older generation was resistant to change because they had seen the ebb and flow of community life from their years of steady faithfulness. They were tired from the tasks of carrying community and longed to hand over the reins. But as soon as something changed, a twinge of discomfort tugged inside.

This is a common challenge for multigenerational churches. But since we were so small, every good and hard thing was amplified. Even so, many of the older members encouraged the younger generations to make things new.

Since the children's play performance was about to begin, we sat down at the tables, already set and arranged. The props and decor were simple: a refrigerator box was a boat draped by a net of multicolored construction paper fish. A blue sheet was the water.

Natalie called the kids forward. The kids, ranging from eighteen months to eight years old, trampled up. Annalee balked at the idea of getting into the cardboard boat with the others; instead, she ran between the boat and me, the soles of her jelly shoes slapping on the speckled linoleum floor as background percussion for the play.

We all knew the ending to this story—not just the story of Jesus and his disciples, but the ending to a cardboard box too full of rowdy children. As they pulled up the heavy net, the cardboard boat felt the supernatural pull of fish. The kids all tipped out, and the box split.

It was a good ending to the new members' first go at a service. And it was a good time to eat that catch of fish.

* * *

No matter how many times we tuned the flute to the guitars, at some point in the worship service, the instruments got pitchy. I winced now and then, sweating from the effort and frustration of projecting my voice and banging my foot along with my guitar strumming, trying to urge our small group to keep time and sing in tune.

At some point in my years of leading worship, the tambourine, the scarves, and the dance moves had emerged from the back closet. I handed instruments out to the kids to play during worship. And believe it or not, I invited every able person to dance—if not with streamers and bells on their socks, then at least with instruments and joy.

By the time the sermon came along, Matthew—who was preaching—was glad for a break from chasing Annalee back and forth behind the semicircle of chairs. I made eye contact with Dave or Natalie, and they swept Annalee up.

As Matthew began to speak, Annalee escaped from the arms that were holding her and ran up to the front, passing in between the chairs, her hair patted by folks of all ages. She tapped a sleeve or a knee, then took off again, this time tottering perilously close to the short table holding the bread and juice for communion. When she reached out to pull the cloth underneath, I put down my guitar and lunged for her, catching her hand just before the juice spilled.

The juice had been poured into a cup made by one of the older members years before, potted with clay from the creek bed in our valley. The widowed, elderly resident, now confined to a wheelchair, preferred not to come to worship anymore, even though his room was only yards from the worship space. He usually just stared out his window, watching the irises grow, looking out for the man who cared for him, for the community members who brought him meals, for the mowers, the mothers, the children, and the seasons that passed across the meadow every day.

He was not with us presently, but we still used his vessel to feast with one another as we passed the bread and the cup in a circle.

I held out my palms to my neighbor. She broke the bread and put it into my hands: "Christiana, this is the body of Christ, broken for you."

"Thanks be to God," I replied.

The bread, which Matthew had baked that morning, was sweet on my tongue. Annalee, fidgeting in my arms, reached for it to taste. I shook my head, wanting her to witness this meal but to wait to participate until she was older. Then I passed the bread along, repeating the words of administration from this saint and sinner to the next.

We washed the bread down with the grape juice, made in the fall from the vines outside the church windows.

This was the feast of victory: when all that was awkward, wounded, joyous, and homemade was passed around, and when Christ's body reminded us why we lived together, why we ate together, and why we worshiped. The meal healed our hurts, mended our fences, and pulled us out of melancholy into the celebration of a mystery both ancient and living. It was a mystery that still surprised us each time we broke bread, scraped off each other's food scraps, and sang in tune.

For a moment, it felt as though we were the church as Christ intended. And it was as miraculous as a heavy catch of fish.

30

Interlude:
Awakening

PERHAPS IT'S NO SURPRISE that Simone Weil's spiritual awakening comes in Assisi, at the church where Saint Francis prayed. For the first time, she lowers herself to her knees in prayer. A year before, in a time of her own physical and spiritual suffering, she encountered the women of a Portuguese fishing village. The simplicity of their faith and their hymn singing make clear to her that she can't help belonging to Christ.[1] It is these mystical experiences of God at Assisi and in the village, along with her contemplation of the crucified Christ and her feeling of the presence of God as she repeats lines from the George Herbert poem "Love"—a poem that has become a prayer for her—that bring Simone to faith in God.

But her route to God has been unusual, unencumbered by the doctrine learned in places of worship. While some could see this as strange and problematic, Simone's encounters with God, free of social or ecclesiastical pressure, can be offered as proof of the power of the simple message of Jesus. For it is in her strivings to live like the poor—like Francis, Dorothy Day, and Clare—that Simone discovers the truth of the gospel.

Simone believed that she never really converted because she had always been a Christian: even though "she had never knelt, she had never prayed, she had never entered a Church,"[2] it seems that God sought and found her.

Her approach to the spiritual life is inspiring but also could be troubling, especially for those committed to the church. Though her friend Father Perrin urges it of her, Simone never allows herself to commit to a church or even to be baptized. Jesus' life has taught her to be wary of these religious traditions and symbols. They are part of a troubling system of power, and by their very nature they exclude rather than include.

Loving his friend and fearing for her soul, Perrin continues to encourage Simone to be baptized. But she is unrelenting. She replies to him in a letter that she will wait for God to convince her to enter the church's doors and become a member. Until God commands her, obedience demands her absence from the church. "If it were conceivable that in obeying God one should bring about one's own damnation while in disobeying him one could be saved," she writes, "I should still choose the way of obedience."[3]

She obeys even until her death.

31

Letter to Simone Weil:
The Miracle of Attention

Dear Simone,

You probably don't remember me, but we've met before. It was only a brief introduction. I was a shy, introverted, and dowdy college student, and well, I guess you were a bit dowdy too. You'd think our affinities would've lead me to soak up your words in *Waiting for God* in my Literature and Belief class during my third year of college.

The difference is that while your outwardly awkward appearance seemed to be intentional, I stumbled into college, desperately hoping I could escape myself and be someone shining and lovely. Maybe that's why your words didn't make sense to me: you were trying to be what I was trying to escape.

But as I've approached you again as an adult who has been humbled and maybe grown a bit wiser, I have a mixed response to you. First, I bristle against your words and ideals. For someone like me who is so committed to the church, your refusal to become a part of the body of Christ troubles me. That's not necessarily a bad thing: I think being troubled is a vital part of reevaluating some of our long-held beliefs. But it does leave me with all sorts of questions. Was God really speaking to you, telling you *not* to be baptized? Are we all supposed to reject community the way you did? Or was it just you?

Simone, I hear a lot from Christians these days who are hoping to find a truly authentic church home. They talk about a certain ideal model of church: it must be open and community oriented, a place where people allow themselves and others to be vulnerable, where the marginalized feel welcome and the sheen of worship doesn't overpower the realness of people, where social justice is celebrated and enemies are prayed for.

I go to that church. I live in that community. There is such beauty and redemption in this church. My children can't wait to go to church. They love it. They love the music we sing, the stories we tell, the way they are included and respected, treated not as an afterthought but as an important part of worship.

But those who hold up this model as the ideal might be surprised to learn that the reality isn't always pretty. Because we are so small and community oriented, the worship can sound crappy. Because we are eager to welcome all and be authentically ourselves, our vulnerability can give off a weird vibe to visitors. And just like other churches, we wound each other, we cause suffering, and sometimes by either action or inaction, we devastate even the most vulnerable among us.

I suspect you knew this was true of our churches, and maybe that's part of why you separated yourself from them. You were a mind ahead of your time and a spiritual mystic genius.

Maybe it's because I'm not a genius that I don't always understand what you say. Your essay on attention mostly baffled me until I came to your prophetic words about prayer.

You lived before the advent of the Internet and smartphones. Yet you understood that the discipline of attention is necessary for prayer. What would you think of our attention spans now, Simone? We are nations of interruptions. Even now, as I type this on my computer, I find that I need a break every fifteen minutes or so to search the web, to think about something else, to do something that takes my attention away from what I'm writing.

On the other hand, I hope you don't take offense from this less intelligent but no less heart-filled woman. I think you worked so hard to be authentic, to be utterly committed to the cause, and to hold fast to the ideals you saw as emanating from Christ himself that you lost sight of the wisdom and discernment of some of your choices. Was it really helping anyone for you to starve to death? Would you take that back if you could?

Something that I've learned from being a mother is that you have to give up your ideals sometimes to care for others. Ideals don't rock a baby to sleep, they don't clean a dirty diaper, they don't help you through the nuances of parental discipline and your own realization of your weaknesses, which are marked with bright flares in the eyes and words of your children. Ideals are all uncluttered corners and angles, obstinate and unwilling to budge. Parenting that way can have disastrous results.

Maybe this is what I've been trying to say, Simone: I respect your absolute commitment, but I cannot follow you there. I have too many people to care for.

But I also have another response to you, a surprising one. And I think it could only come after some suffering, some challenges, and some maturity. It goes back to that essay on attention. You talk about the physical struggle, the "muscular effort" it takes to focus attention, even on seemingly innocuous things like geometry. You say that "attention consists of suspending our thought, leaving it detached and empty. . . . Above all our thoughts should be empty, waiting, not seeking anything, but ready to receive in its naked truth the object that is to penetrate it."[1]

You could almost be speaking of the ever-changing nature of parenting, or at least the openness parents must have to the complexities of their children's needs. But then I wonder if you are referring here to the mechanism of meditation and contemplative prayer, that they aren't ends unto themselves. And just when I think I have you pegged, you knock me over the head with your point: "Not only does the love of God have attention for its substance; the love of our neighbor, which we know to be the same love, is made of the same substance. Those who are unhappy have no need for anything in this world but people capable of giving them their attention. The capacity to give one's attention to a sufferer is a very rare and difficult thing . . . it *is* a miracle."[2]

Oh, Simone, you got it all along, didn't you: the utter miracle of love.

You say: "The love of our neighbor in all its fullness simply means being able to say to him: 'What are you going through?'"[3]

I am terrible at this, I confess. Because it's so hard. The unhappiest people are that way because they were not loved well or taught how to love. We must know ourselves, our faults, sins, and weaknesses, and know that even with all our shadows, we are loved by God, in order to look at someone else and ask, "What are you going through?"

Maybe that is why I'm not so good at this yet, Simone. I am digging up the darkness inside me, uncovering my shadows, looking at them one by one, and am trying to see that God loves and accepts me even there. I want so much to love others well, but it takes energy and a kind of discipline, yes, attention, that I never anticipated.

Your words have been discomfiting. But I see now that in many ways, you understand more than I do. And I confess that I am defensive because you have poked at my weakness.

Still, I wonder what you would do if you appeared in our community. We aren't the church of the 1940s that you were so wary of joining. If you ever want to come visit our ragtag group, I promise to listen to you with an open heart. I won't agree with everything you say, but I wonder if our community might change your mind a bit. Would you consider joining us? We are seeking the truth too.

Your friend,

Christiana

PART V

DEATH

Praise to you, O my Lord, for our Sister Death
and the death of the body from whom
no one may escape.

—Saint Francis of Assisi, "Canticle of the
Creatures"

32

Broken Things

A FEW MONTHS after our vacation in Colorado during which Dad told us about his cancer, I traveled back to Texas. Trained by years of overseas travel in my twenties—and having lost enough luggage along the way—I had taken very little with me on the trip: my carry-on, my diaper bag, and Annalee.

My older sister, Heatherly, met me in baggage claim. I regret to admit that I usually take some pride in meeting my family in baggage claim and hearing one of them say, "This is all you brought?" But this time my baggage, of another sort, was heavier than any suitcase I could pack. Heatherly hugged me and took my luggage. I thanked her for picking me up, and until we got to the car, we didn't talk much about our parents. Usually it was Mom, in a brightly colored scarf, a patterned dress, and narrow flats, who would greet me at the airport. But now she was three hours away at a hospital in Houston with my father.

The tumor in Dad's L2 vertebrae, the one that had been bothering him in Colorado, had deteriorated and cracked his bone; shards of bone were piercing him internally. He was in so much pain that he couldn't even sit up straight enough to have any sort of treatment. Trapped in the claustrophobic stillness of an MRI was agonizing. So he was going into surgery soon.

I realize now just how fortunate I am that my parents' house felt like home for so many years. Mom's greatest joy has always been her children and grandchildren. That meant that because my family and I were the only ones who lived out of town, when we visited Mom put all her love into making our spaces, the food we ate, and the company we kept as comforting and pleasant as possible.

My mom's absence at the airport and the fact that I would be staying at Heatherly's house instead of hers was a small grief in the big scheme of things. But piled on top of unknowns about my father's health and my lingering anxiety, the shimmering sheen of home had finally been rubbed down into a dull reality.

Although I assumed I would be able to see Dad during the long weekend I was in Texas, I was here for a different task. Heatherly, Elena, and Mom had recently moved my grandmother (Dad's mother, Mimi) into an assisted living apartment because of her dementia. For years, they had walked the delicate balance of elder care, offering dignity and respect to my grandmother for as long as possible before she stopped bathing herself, felt afraid to be alone, and couldn't remember to pay her bills or answer the phone.

I was here to do my small part: to help my sisters go through Mimi's house. When we entered our grandmother's home, I thought to myself, "Thank goodness I have such a small house. I don't need any of this." Even so, when I opened my first old trunk, filled with family heirlooms, untold stories, and secret facts and facets of my ancestors, I felt the thrill of the hunt.

I lifted yellowed tissue paper and unwrapped my father's neatly folded baby clothes. Each layer underneath unearthed another ancestor's possessions: my grandmother's childhood nightclothes, her sister's fancy gloves, my great-grandmother's farm bonnet, my great-great-grandmother's handmade dresses.

My saintly sisters were entering their third week of organizing the chaos that was our grandmother's home. Where I was still enthusiastic, they found the fantasy of a treasure hunt to be wearing thin. A few hours into the hunt, the dust began to smell to me too. There were boxes and boxes of greeting cards, some from the 1970s, albums full of postcards, and a small bag of my father's baby hair. After the third coin purse from the 1930s that disintegrated in our hands, fascination had literally given me a headache.

Everything was hand labeled in neat cursive, and even old letters were summarized on the envelopes. I could picture my grandmother—widowed twice, the last of her siblings, the family keeper with only one son to pass things down to—reading her memories, packing them away into boxes, weeping alone.

She was largely unable to impart them to us, her granddaughters, as if sharing them would take the memories away from her or reveal too much of her heartaches. As we went through her things, I think we were also attempting to access parts of my father's childhood, longing to know who his mother was, who our father was, who we were.

With each box and picture, we uncovered grief. We grieved for our father's physical pain. We grieved for the things that kept our grandmother from being free from memories that wounded her. We grieved for the pain of life and the inevitability of death and for the lies we believed about ourselves and each other as children, lies that sometimes kept us from joy.

With every picture of my young chubby self, I remembered the self-loathing I felt all throughout my childhood. As an adult and a parent of young children, though, I suddenly felt a new affection for the child in those photos, a child who was sensitive to so many things, who thought she should be different, who was no more awkward than the classmates, friends, and family who populated the pictures around her. Pictures of Heatherly, who was my beautiful older sister, the one I compared myself to as a child, made me sad. As an adult, I could see that she was just a tired teenager then, one trying to cope with her own insecurities and sorrows.

Those evenings, after scouring Mimi's house, Heatherly and I watched stupid movies at her house, being sisters the way we hadn't been in a long time. Maybe there was healing in recognizing our old selves and seeing them and each other anew.

Near the end of the week, the three of us sisters, weary from packing, looked at each other. Then we looked at all our grandmother's old, ugly crystal and glass knickknacks—the ones we'd grown up with but that wouldn't be worth anything to anyone but us—and we grabbed a box of them to take out to the backyard. Each of us chose our favorite ugly squirrel, frilly dancing princess, redbird, or Austrian girl in a dirndl, and we used them as therapy against the brick wall.

Opaque glass of all colors became shards all over the back porch. We shouted and hooted and vowed never to tell our father what we'd done.

* * *

When Elena called me from Texas, I could hear something in her voice. Her first words displayed the intricate weaving of a lifetime of shared familial meaning. At first, I thought she was going to confirm that our grandmother Mimi, who had been on hospice for a few weeks, had died, or that there was something urgent with Dad's health. It had been nearly a year since his cancer diagnosis, and he was proving to be an unusual case for his oncologists. His cancer wasn't progressing as quickly as was anticipated.

But this time, it was Heatherly.

"She's in the ER," Elena said.

I thought I didn't hear her correctly: "Wait. Heatherly is in the emergency room?"

"Yes," Elena said, with characteristic gentleness. "But it's probably just a panic attack."

Panic is such a mild word for the overpowering sense of falling into darkness and fear that comes with such an episode. *Panic* sounds as if it could be washed away with a cup of tea and a warm bubble bath. In the last few years of age, grief, and life transitions, all three of us sisters had become intimate with such darkness. I had groaned for her when my little sister told me that she'd begun having panic attacks, but we had tugged in tightly together and held on, glad that we could at least find solace in knowing what the other was going through. And Heatherly was saddled with the burden of being the oldest daughter in a family struggling through the complexities of cancer and dementia, and having one of her four teens heading off to college.

But this was something worse than even panic. At midnight, another call came from our mother.

"Honey," Mom said, "Heatherly has had a stroke."

Suddenly the litany of terrible things I'd only imagined could happen finally had. The things I had feared in those darkest moments of panic—pain, sickness, and death—were all possible. Though my dad had improved after surgery, he and my grandmother were still ill, the community was struggling, and now my sister had had a stroke at the age of forty.

While her teenage daughters called 911, trying to keep her alert before they arrived, her husband, my parents, and her friends from church rushed to meet Heatherly at the hospital. I was far away in the Midwest, only able to imagine how she felt, how she looked in that hospital bed. In the next few weeks and months, her brain, traumatized by the blood clot that had reached it, left her with confusion, numbness, and pain. She temporarily lost the use of her hand, and even though her speech slowly returned, the whole right side of her body was numb.

I got the updates via text; her friends came to cheer her up. Her kids' youth pastor shared her progress with her listening, prayerful world. Even though I was grateful that so many people were surrounding her, I wanted to be the one sitting beside her. I wanted to fight for her the same way she had for me when we were younger, whether it was chewing out my middle school boyfriend who broke up with me by mail, defending me against a junior high mean girl, or coming to my apartment in the middle of the night when I was living alone and was sick and scared.

I felt that I was failing my sister as I sat a thousand miles away, my prayers, tears, and words the only things I had to offer.

But this stroke didn't unmake her, even when her hands and body were moving without her consent. Slowly, she began to recover.

But a week later, I got the call that our grandmother had died. One grief passed to another.

33

Interlude:
Between the Angel and the Lady

*M*YSTICAL things seem to happen on mountaintops. In the middle of his ministry, Francis and his followers are given the craggy mountaintop of La Verna in Tuscany by a wealthy count who admires his preaching. Although he has relinquished the life of complete solitude that a hermit might lead, Francis still finds time to rest and pray in that place overlooking the isolated valley of Casentino.

A decade later, at the age of forty-three, Francis sets out with Brother Leo and a few others to traverse the steep rocky paths, passing through forests of spruce and beech trees, between mossy overhangs and walls of stone, to the little cells on the mountaintop built for them to fast and pray.

On the way, Francis is tormented by demons, and is so weakened in body and mind that his faithful brothers find a man who offers them his donkey so that Francis might be carried up the mountain. With great turmoil and anguish, they come to La Verna, and Francis gives instructions to his brothers to prepare for their forty-day fast. Every year, in his devotion to both Mary and the archangel Michael, Francis observes the forty days between the Feast of the Assumption of Mary and the Feast of Michael the Archangel.

Maybe Mary and Michael each represent the parts of Francis that he is able to hold on to, even with his devotion to the simple way. In Catholic tradition, the Feast of the Assumption celebrates when Mary's body is drawn into heaven at the end of her life. Does Mary—the girl who in her first spiritual song speaks of her own humility, of the God who scatters the proud, feeds the hungry, lifts up the lowly, and sends the rich away empty handed—does she remind Francis of his first love, Lady Poverty?

And what about the Archangel? As the chief opponent of Satan, the Archangel Michael is a fierce figure in the Catholic tradition, one who shows up at the hour of death and leads the dead to their place of judgment. In Revelation, he battles and defeats the dragon, "that ancient serpent called the devil, or Satan," hurling him and his angels out of heaven to wreak havoc on the earth (Revelation 12:7-9). Is Francis's boyhood fascination with Saint George and the dragon tweaked by the stories of the avenging warrior angel who battles a dragon for God Almighty?

Francis tells his brothers that he knows something about what is to come as he ascends the mountain. He prays: "Lord God, what after my death shall become of Thy mendicant family? . . . Who shall console them? Who shall correct them? Who shall pray to Thee for them?" He worries that when he dies, those who are left will not hold fast to the most important aspects of the brotherhood. An angel assures him: "I tell thee in God's name that the profession of thy Order shall not fail until the Day of Judgment."[1]

With this comfort that the brotherhood will not die, he observes the Feast of the Assumption, contemplating the end of Mary's life. Then he begins his fast, looking toward the end of those forty days when he will celebrate the mighty angel present at death.

But what mysteries and miracles will be performed in between?

34

Our Sacred Cows

THE MORNING after the most intense election many of my generation had ever experienced, I drove Annalee to daycare, feeling weary from the grief and stress in my life as well as the anxiety, the contentiousness, the racism, the bigotry, and the hatred in our country. I had taken to praying with a Franciscan rosary I bought on a recent trip to the town in New Mexico named for Francis: Santa Fe. I confess that I didn't know how to pray a proper Rosary. My daughter had tried to teach me the Rosary she learned in Catholic school. But I fumbled along and ended up using the beads as a way to string my prayers together, to chant them in a meditative way that kept my mind and body absorbed in the prayers. I unhooked the rosary from the rearview mirror, where its light wooden beads dangled most days. And I began to pray, "Lord have mercy, Christ have mercy," while naming our country, our electorate, the voters, the candidates, our local towns, Plow Creek, each family, and my sister and father. When I got to some of our neighbors at Plow Creek, I paused.

On a recent family trip to Kentucky, Matthew and I had taken our kids to visit the historical Shaker village of Pleasant Hill outside of Lexington. Set on thousands of acres where stone fences reminiscent of Hadrian's Wall lined the edges of fields, the sprawling community was started in the 1800s. Shakerism (as it was later named by confused and sometimes scandalized outsiders because of the community's worship services: raucous and exuberant sounds like thunder for miles around) was begun by a religious group who broke off from the Quakers. One of the early converts, a poor and illiterate factory worker from England named Ann Lee, became one of its leaders and prophets. Eventually, Ann and a few followers moved to America to find religious freedom for their movement. The movement spread quickly, and dozens of communities built their numbers to nearly six thousand at its peak. One of its original communities, Pleasant Hill was a beautiful village that once housed about five hundred members. The community was made up of celibate men and women who adopted children they raised together.

The community continued until the early 1900s, when it finally dissolved because of dwindling numbers.

As we began our guided tour of the grounds, Matthew commented that the village reminded him of Plow Creek. I scoffed. How could a village that required celibacy and separate living quarters for men and women be much like our Mennonite community? But as we continued our tour and heard tales of their belief that work was a gift from God, of their construction of the surrounding structures by hand, of their communal living, pacifism, dancing in worship, and radical views on the equality of all people—no matter their gender, ethnicity, or economic background—well, their ideals began to sound familiar. That the Shakers had farmed sustainably for two hundred years settled it. Matthew was right: we did have some things in common with the Shakers.

For the next few hours, we joked about traveling to Maine, where the only active Shaker community still existed. The kids weren't too keen on the idea of being raised in separate quarters from their parents. And I'm not sure who was less excited about living as brother and sister: Matthew or me.

We took a tour through the small farming operation that honored the Shaker model of sustainable care for the earth. The farm grew food for the bed-and-breakfast and restaurant on the premises. While I supervised the kids as they petted the animals, Matthew couldn't seem to pull himself away from the crops. After giving everything to build up the farm, this was what he knew best.

But Plow Creek's farm had been flailing of late. Even after just finishing one of the most profitable farm seasons, Matthew was still struggling to make a living wage.

As I continued to pray with my rosary on the drive to Annalee's daycare, I thought about the Sunday before, when we'd sat in church at Plow Creek, shocked and discouraged by the lack of congregants. Only eight adults had shown up: all the older folks and our young family.

Natalie and Allan, the newly married couple who had helped out on the farm for years, had recently decided to move to another community, and we were all a bit demoralized. Their vibrancy was an antidote to the natural melancholy of our community members. The interns had all left for the season. And we knew that winter, with its forced, lonely, months-long Sabbath, was upon us.

That Sunday evening, the most recent couple to move to the community invited us for dinner. They had joined Plow Creek a few years before. The husband was in leadership with Matthew, and together they'd helped implement a new visioning process, one that had begun to finally give us hope for the future of Plow Creek. The wife was a hard and focused worker on the farm with Matthew, and she had helped rebuild a successful CSA (community-supported agriculture) program on the farm. We thought their dinner invitation was offered to lend support during a stressful time for us. We had just found out that we were unexpectedly pregnant with our fourth child. Mixed in with this surprise were my grief and anxiety over my dad's and sister's health and my grandmother's death. Matthew and I both felt weary and overwhelmed.

But they'd invited us over to say that they were moving. They'd decided it was too difficult to keep living at Plow Creek, and it was time for them to leave. They were worried we'd be angry with them or storm out. But the truth was, I understood. Completely. I knew how it felt to need some relief from the overwhelming weariness of life. Of trying over and over to make things work even when they weren't.

But even with that understanding, Matthew and I went home shell-shocked. Because this young family had been so involved in many aspects of Plow Creek, we knew their departure meant that the leadership and finances were going to suffer. The farm Matthew had worked so hard to build up—which had just had its best year in a long time—would be losing several of its strongest workers. We'd all been working so hard to build up the community over the past many years, forming new leadership structures and making new traditions. But what was happening? People were still unable or unwilling to stay. We were tired already. What did this mean for all of us, for the community, that we couldn't keep another family?

I told Matthew that night: I'm tired already, and this just means more work put back on the rest of us. How is the community going to cope with this? How are *we* going to cope?

On that drive to daycare, as I hesitated in prayer for the older members of Plow Creek, I was struck with an intense feeling: What happens to them if the community crumbles? Was it our duty as their brothers and sisters to sacrifice a bit more to care for them, to continue holding on to these structures when they weren't as fruitful as we'd hoped?

Clare of Assisi knew that "poverty frees us from the selfishness that binds our lives" and we are then more vulnerable, and therefore more open to allowing God to be present in our lives.[1] Because we had education, resources, and the help of extended family, we would never be truly poor. Yet, it felt as though God was allowing us to experience a measure of spiritual poverty.

Matthew's farming vocation was looking bleaker, and our community was dwindling. Having no maternity insurance, we were expecting a baby, and my family members were struggling with ill health. Our ideals were being flattened, and we truly didn't have any idea which way to go.

* * *

As we drove up to the Plow Creek common building one Saturday morning, cars overflowed from the small gravel lot in front and were parked on the grass all the way around the edges of the large circular meadow. The only time I'd seen this many people at the community was for Natalie and Allan's wedding the summer before.

But these cars were here for another major event: a funeral.

David—the man who had handed over the $10,000 to buy the 180-acre property in the 1970s—had died peacefully in his sleep. He and his wife, Margaret, were the longest-standing members of the community. David was a self-taught carpenter and builder, and his handiwork was evident all over the property, in every building and structure he'd helped construct.

We parked across the meadow and walked toward the common building—another structure that had David's fingerprints all over it—where the funeral was being held. The windows were fogging up and the backs of funeral guests lined the windows, a telltale sign of a crowded room. When we entered, it was standing room only.

Because I was expecting our fourth child, a kind friend gave up his chair for me, and I found myself sitting beside a woman a few years younger than me who had grown up at Plow Creek.

Her parents, longtime members of the community, had moved away not long after we first arrived at Plow Creek. She and I were vague acquaintances, and we talked briefly before the service. For those of us who were current members, this number of people was unusual. I asked her if the gathering seemed to her like a large group of people at Plow Creek. She had grown up during something of a heyday in Plow Creek's history: the 1980s and early 1990s, when membership soared to nearly a hundred people.

She shook her head. "Oh, not at all," she told me. "At my baptism, there were people seated in a circle, three rows deep."

As I looked around at the crowd, about a quarter of whom I recognized, I realized that these people represented the history of Plow Creek. Many had grown up or spent a good part of their married lives in the community. And as people were invited to speak about David, a collective narrative—one that I'd heard in snippets throughout our seven years—emerged: one of growth, life, meaning, peace, and faithfulness. The stories of David's courage in pacifism, his quiet humility in teaching himself so many skills that were essential for the building up of community, and his stern attention to safety, combined with the way he encouraged his five children's adventurous spirits, brought a mix of emotions for me.

Matthew and I hadn't known very well the David they were speaking of. He was slowing down by the time we moved to Plow Creek, and a year or two later he had a stroke that weakened his body and memory. But what unsettled me the most was that we didn't know the community that many of these guests were speaking about. It was clear that Plow Creek was not what it once was.

The people who came with David and Margaret in the 1970s had brought with them a tremendous energy and passion for building community. They built and created their spaces, homes, and resources from scratch. They had arrived with a unified vision that centered on sharing their lives together, finances and all.

Because of their hard work, these forty years later, we had all the resources and infrastructure we needed. But the vision of sharing finances had fallen away, and we lacked the energy to help the community grow and continue. We'd lost two families in the past few months, and while I was sad, I hadn't blamed them. Part of me was actually jealous that they'd made such clean and determined decisions. With much effort at recreating new structures to shore up the ones that were crumbling, we'd seen the community grow in the past three years. And then, somewhat suddenly, it had begun to decline again.

I felt weary in a floundering community, and I didn't know if I had the energy to build onto a vision that didn't seem to excite anyone new. I wasn't arrogant enough to think it could ever be totally my fault, but I wondered if I was partly to blame—if my lack of love for my neighbor and my inability to live more simply, to show deeper hospitality, to develop a stronger contemplative life, to live into the poverty of life in Christ, had made it harder for the place to grow. I felt there was meaning in staying when it was hard, even through the struggle. But I needed more life and joy. I needed to really feel that there was still meaning in this way of being church together.

I couldn't help but feel that we were just spinning our wheels. And I realized that, like the last Shaker inhabitants who stayed at Pleasant Hill even after everyone else had left or died, the older folks might want to wait out the end.

But I wasn't sure I wanted to join them.

* * *

We were all dreading the community meeting. This kind of dread before a meeting wasn't anything new for me. Because of the slowing season for our farm and bakery workers, our community meetings became more focused in the winter. During the height of my anxiety, I used to breathe through those community meetings, heat flaring through my face and shoulders as the telltale sign of a panic attack.

Though my anxiety had settled down during the last year, I still loathed these meetings. This was likely the residue of the old anxieties that would emerge with any sort of tension or conflict. Though the largest conflicts over the years had been mostly worked through, a voice or two usually expressed dissent to what seemed, to the rest of us, like wise ideas for moving forward.

But this meeting felt particularly fraught. It was our first since the two families had decided to leave, since David had died, and since our most elderly member, Jim, had been placed on hospice care. Our numbers were shrinking, and an already weary group knew that the tasks of making such a large property work properly would not go away. We were all feeling the intensity and knew it might rise up during a tense meeting.

We gathered to eat pizza at the common building before the meeting. The kids, thrilled to be staying up late on a school night, took turns dragging each other across the linoleum floor, plunking random notes on the piano in the room, sneaking cookies, and chasing each other. I had the suspicion that, like me, the other parents were glad to be preoccupied with our children—anything to put off starting the meeting. When we finally got the kids corralled into the back playroom, our meeting began.

We prayed and sang together Jim Croegaert's "House of Peace":

> You have brought us so very far in so short a time
> In spite of all our weaknesses, in spite of all our crying
> You are worthy of everything, every word of praise
> Every song we will ever sing, fountain of all grace
> Our High Priest,
> Make us a House of Peace

I believe we all truly wanted Plow Creek to be defined, among other good qualities, as a place where peace was lived out in our daily lives.

As the meeting began and we went around the circle, listening to every person's feelings about our recent losses, I had to admit that I was glad Matthew and I weren't the only ones who were discouraged. I shared with the group that I was weary and disheartened. But what I wasn't yet ready to say was that I was worried that things would just continue to drag on as they had been for years. That we would leave just so we wouldn't have to watch Plow Creek die a slow and sad death the way the Shaker village had.

After we heard how everyone felt, we began to share our hopes and visions for the future of Plow Creek. It was clear that many of the older people had hope. I sunk lower in my chair, my insides starting to shake with the old dustings of anxiety. A large part of me didn't want them to feel hope. I wanted them to feel what Matthew and I felt: tapped out, overwhelmed, in need of a change.

But the refrain continued. Even in the midst of their grief and discouragement, many of the folks around the circle repeated the words that we'd heard off and on when issues arose at Plow Creek: "God will provide more people." "God is faithful; we just need to be faithful too."

Sometimes these meetings felt to me like the large flock of blackbirds I would see on our road. On walks I sometimes called out to them so they would rise from their resting spots in the tips of the trees, and I delighted when the sound of my car nearing their safe space startled them and they took flight. They would rise into the air like an oratorio, gliding one way in harmony and then suddenly shifting to another movement and flying in another direction as one.

It was as if each of these meetings needed to start with all of us resting in the spaces of the trees. But there was often a moment of shifting—either a great rising out of the trees or a sudden change of course.

When Dave Bell, the farmer who loved Annalee so much, spoke that night, the course shifted, and I was grateful that some hard truths began to be spoken. "I wish I felt as hopeful, but I don't have a lot of hope," Dave said. "I understand why families have left. Maybe there's hope, but I can't see how it can keep going the way it's going and last much longer. Without something of a vision that everyone wants to buy into—and everyone has to buy into it—it's never going to work. I'm really disheartened."

As Matthew spoke next, his eyes were bright with passion but his expression was so weary it made me want to weep. "I have some hope that comes from being here eight years and seeing people take obedience to Jesus radically and seriously," he said. "I've been extremely thankful. But there have to be really big changes. And I have to be honest: my tank is empty, and I just don't have any more to give. If this community is to continue, we are each going to have to be willing to let our sacred cows die, whether that be the church, the farm, the bakery, or the common purse. I include myself in this. But our sacred cows need to die."

"Well, let's take them to the butcher," interjected Sarah with a laugh. Sarah was a member in her sixties who'd lived here since before I was born. Her husband, Rich, was an elder who, despite being confined to a wheelchair because of rheumatoid arthritis that began when he was sixteen, had been a loving leader at Plow Creek for thirty years, but he hadn't been able to make the meeting because of a decline in his health. Tears began to slip out from behind Sarah's glasses.

"I was resonating with Matthew's idea: everything has to die to start again," Sarah said. "In my grief, it seemed kind of appropriate that we realized at David's funeral—the guy who put the money down for the property—that Plow Creek seems to be dying with him. My hope comes from the Lord, who made heaven and earth. As far as the details, I can't put it into words."

"That's just the way I felt, Sarah," I said. "I realized that the community that existed for those who came to honor and remember David at his funeral and share their memories of Plow Creek—well, that community is also dead."

For decades, the Plow Creek vision of "a global village practicing the peace of Jesus" had been a good goal. But it no longer characterized our community. Even though through the years we'd enjoyed community with people of different nationalities and ethnicities, we weren't "global" anymore. True, our backgrounds and ages were diverse (and we had children of color among us), but those of us sitting in that meeting were a group of white adults. Was our lack of diversity just one symptom of our bigger problems? Had we become so insular that we couldn't be community to anyone besides people like ourselves?

We needed a new vision we believed in, one that could open us up to growing and learning and serving others different from ourselves.

When Mark, an older member who had encouraged me to join the music team, declared that the community of the

1980s and 1990s was dead, it seemed as if the flock of birds flew into the distance.

Finally, everyone seemed to be on the same page.

35

Hospice

THAT MY DAD'S health was worsening, despite the early optimism of his oncologists, was a fact I'd been able to avoid by living so far away from my family. I didn't understand how badly my father's health had declined until I went to Texas for Christmas. And it took several days after we got there before we even were able to see Dad. I was shocked to learn that even though they all lived within miles of each other, Heatherly and Elena hadn't even seen him since Thanksgiving. It wasn't from their lack of desire but from Dad's determination to be sick without any intrusion. A few days into our trip, Mom told us to come over. Dad might or might not come out of his room, she told us, but we could sit in the living room and visit, hoping that he would.

When my dad first appeared through the door of his bedroom, I glimpsed his mother in his face and the way he moved his body. But it wasn't a sweet resemblance that one might note about family members. He reminded me of Mimi in her last days of dementia at ninety years old, mouth slack from the lost muscle mass of aging. Dad had lost a shocking amount of weight.

"Hi, Daddy," Heatherly said. He lifted several smooth, elegant fingers in response, a gesture that could have been either a reflex or a sagging, slow signal of strength, performed with agonizing effort, in front of his daughters. But he clearly had no strength. Every step and movement was painful.

Mom uncurled her legs from her seat to lead him to the high-backed chair that faced us, his three daughters, who had been waiting to see him.

He shuffled forward, his back curved from the pain of the cancer in his bones. He was dressed in an old sweatshirt from my alma mater, which I'd given him when I was in college. In big flannel letters, it said "Dad." The color scheme was circa the late 1990s. No one wore white sweatshirts anymore, especially with such loudly stitched letters. But his outfit, along with bright red pajama pants, was a poignant nod to days long past. When we were teenagers, sometimes he would emerge from that back bedroom in intentionally ridiculous outfits—a baseball cap with a fake ponytail, white shorts just a tad too short, loud Hawaiian shirts—usually just to see how a nervous boyfriend trying to impress his girlfriend's dad would react.

But although we commented on his outfit in an effort to approach a heavy situation with some levity, none of us felt like laughing. Even the sweatshirt couldn't hide the fact that he was extremely thin. His normally robust frame was frail, and his mouth was so restricted from pain that any words spoken sounded like the garbled texture of an elderly person.

I wonder if Mom noticed our shock. Unlike her, we hadn't seen his decline so closely, day by day.

Once he was seated, we waited for him to speak. We knew his speech was limited because of a blockage in his esophagus, but our waiting was also an old habit, born of years of learning how to communicate with a father who resisted answering questions, who preferred to do the asking himself. A conversation with anyone else in his position would have begun with one of us asking how he was doing, how he was feeling, how his pain level was. But what could we say to the man who had always controlled the conversation?

After a few quiet moments, he declared in a muffled, scratchy voice, "Don't sit around talking about me when I'm unconscious."

We were stunned by both the abruptness of his non sequitur and the words themselves. I'd longed for a sweet interaction with him, in which we'd talk of love and memory, and in which I'd share with him my gratitude that I'd had him as a father, and in which he would call me "baby" and tell me he was proud of me. I longed for things that I hadn't thought I needed from him anymore. It was as if his proximity to death brought me back to my deepest needs in the hollows of my childhood.

"Can we read to you, then?" Elena asked.

"No."

"What about singing? Can we gather and sing to you?" I asked.

He shook his head. No, he didn't want any clichéd endings, no platitudes, no deathbed goodbyes.

What else was there to say?

We chatted around him as he fidgeted in his seat. He was visibly uncomfortable, and I wondered if his outburst was out of some delirium born of dehydration. Clearly, his pain and illness had left him depleted in every way. Was it right to blame him? Still, his outburst had hurt.

After a visit to the oncologist a few days later, which Dad could hardly stand because of the pain, they sent him straight to the hospital for IV fluids. His hospital stay necessitated pain medication and scans. When the surgeons couldn't place a feeding tube down his throat, they soon understood the truth: the cancer had crawled up his esophagus and was blocking his throat. A feeding tube would need to be inserted straight into his stomach.

While Mom and Dad spent their days and nights at the hospital, the rest of us celebrated, more or less, Christmas and the New Year together. We did all the things my family wasn't able to do in our rural life. We ordered in Mexican food, played card games, drank coffee from a Keurig after dinner, ate Indian food, and watched the supremely depressing countdown to the new year with Ryan Seacrest.

We wondered if we should feel guilty about being together doing these things while Mom and Dad were stuck in the hospital. It's true that our family was used to celebrating while Dad hovered on the fringes. These were extreme circumstances, yes. But in some ways, Dad had spent our lives intentionally trying to make it easier for us to be without him.

My mom was so insistent on protecting my dad's privacy that it wasn't as though we could come over and offer him any small bits of celebration. Except for a few allowed visits, when we brought meals to the hospital for Mom, she met us in the lobby to get them. She said the smell bothered Dad. But the truth was, he didn't want anyone there except for her. Sometimes even her presence seemed to disturb him.

A large part of me understood his need for solitude. I was like him in many ways: high on the introvert scale, moody, introspective. I couldn't help that I craved solitude on days when my house and the community felt chaotic. I couldn't help that any more than my dad could help the fact that being with people drained energy that he just didn't have.

But his deep emotional privacy was something that we didn't share, and it was something that hurt me. Until I saw him that day in the living room, I'd thought I'd stopped longing for his effusive affection, that I didn't really need it anymore. But I found that in order to grieve, I had to accept some things. Though I knew he loved me, it saddened me that he was never able to give me what I needed emotionally.

It was becoming clear that the loss of a loved one wasn't going to be as simple as sadness. This grief was unearthing long-buried hurts and unmet needs. It was clarifying each of our failings.

* * *

When the hospice nurse and social worker came to my parents' home the first time, they were not what my sisters and I expected. Is there a cliché for what a hospice care provider is supposed to be like? I thought they'd be calm and restful sorts, hired because of their ability to show quiet dignity to patients who are dying. Instead, they were chatty and gregarious. But there was a charm and assurance to their lack of worry about being so close to death; surely they also needed a way to cope with the heavy burden of their job.

They were kind and highly knowledgeable, but they rushed my mom through the heavy information about signing "do not resuscitate at home" forms, the different kinds of pain management options, and noticing the stages before death. The nurse enthusiastically declared that she used to be afraid of morphine but loved it now because of the relief it offered suffering patients. I suppose it could seem jarring to someone newly acquainted with hospice care, but I think it was necessary for my mom to hear. She was afraid of giving my father too much pain medication— afraid she'd accidentally be the one to kill him, instead of the cancer.

My mom had needed help ever since Dad came home from the hospital. She needed help caring for his bedsores, managing his pain, and dealing with the emotional weight of acknowledging that he wasn't going to recover. Annalee and I had spent an extra two weeks with them in Texas after Christmas. The sound of a mini vacuum became familiar throughout the house as it suctioned the saliva and mucus from Dad's throat. He could no longer swallow and required a machine to do what most of us take for granted.

My mom put her head down at some point in the three-hour hospice meeting, covering her face with both hands, running them over her hair and tossing it about as if that would shake out the grief for a moment so she could think. I could see that she was becoming more and more overwhelmed by the information and emotional weight of deciding to place my dad on hospice.

Meanwhile, I got a call from Plow Creek where Matthew was caring for Neva and Jude so I could be there for my mom. Our elder Rich—who had been the heart of our small intentional community for thirty years—had also been placed on hospice.

His wife, Sarah, a career nurse, was giving him morphine under the tongue. While my dad couldn't swallow anymore because of the cancer that was creeping up his throat, it was Rich's diseased lungs that would fill with fluid until he couldn't breathe any longer.

Later, Sarah and I would swap morphine and hospice stories. But while I was in Texas, the two wives in their sixties (my mom and Sarah) woke and slept fitfully to the tune of grief and dying.

A few days before I returned home, I got the message that Rich had died. His death was a big blow to the community, one that had lost two other elderly members in a few months. Although I longed to be with my husband and kids, I was dreading the return. The day after I got home, Matthew would lead Rich's funeral.

I felt as though I was traveling from grief to grief, from my father on hospice to a community of loss. It was a community that seemed to be fraying, a community that might need hospice care itself.

I'd never lost a father before, so I didn't know what his death would be like. But now it seemed that dying was a harsher master than death. It refused to follow a set pattern. This kind of slow dying actually complicated death—not because we always wanted death to come but because dying was filled with the looming shadow of dread.

I dreaded the death of my father. But I also dreaded his prolonged suffering.

And my small community that lingered on in triage—I dreaded to watch it flounder, to watch it waste away to a shell as thin as my father's frame.

One day when the hospice nurse returned from examining my father in his bedroom, she seemed uncharacteristically exasperated. "I asked him, out of ten, what his pain level was, and he told me a two," she said. "A *two!*"

It was almost funny. My dad's unwillingness or inability to own up to his suffering was at once baffling and also utterly predictable. I sometimes wondered if he feared the loss of control more than the actual pain.

"At least he gave you a number," one of us said. "In the hospital, when a nurse would ask him how he was feeling, he'd just say, 'I'm very blessed.'"

"Well, I don't care what he says. I'm writing down a seven," the nurse declared. "I can tell that man is in a lot of pain."

My mom nodded wearily, knowingly.

"You've been giving him enough for a hangnail," the nurse said to my mother. "You can give him a lot more than that."

The dread was a wave that filled and emptied us as it willed. But there was hope for my mom, for my dad, in that little offering from the nurse. That instruction for pain relief pushed the wave away, at least for a brief respite.

What we all expressed, what we all wanted for my dad, for Rich, for the community, was an end to suffering. Even if it was at the bottom of a vial of morphine, at the end of dying, at the last breath of a community.

But I wondered too: Was there an offering in the dread itself, in the dark shape that followed as close as a shadow? If Thomas Merton was to be believed, the pit that is dug by dread is a prerequisite for the healing of God. Maybe it's naïveté that made me hope that this season of dread would bring something besides death.

"The liturgy, which is his joy and which reveals to him the glory of God, cannot fill a heart that has not previously been humbled and emptied by dread," wrote Merton. "*Alleluia* is the song of the desert."[1]

But by then, would we all be too exhausted to sing alleluia in the desert? Or would God mind that, sometimes, the song of praise is as quiet as a puff of sand in the wind?

36

Interlude:
A Broken Body

*F*OR DAYS, the demons torment Francis on the mountaintop of La Verna, nearly knocking him off the cliff face to his death. The hunger pains in his belly cannot be as bad as his mental anguish. Is he tempted to call out for his beloved Brother Leo, the only brother who truly understands his need for solitude? Leo is the one who hovers close enough to hear him the moment his spiritual father needs him, and he is the one close enough to witness Francis's vision of flames that descend from the heavens to rest atop his head.

Exhausted from hunger, from the beating and accusations of the demons, from a life of self-abnegation, Francis prays that God will be merciful to him. God answers, preparing him for what is soon to come, preparing him for the confusing and complex mixture of joy, pain, sorrow, and love he will soon feel.

Before he begins his passionate contemplation once more, Francis prays that he will be given the gift of understanding both the pain of Jesus' passion on the cross and the "exceeding love, whereby Thou, Son of God, wast enkindled to willingly bear such passion for us."[1] Then, like his beloved Clare, he contemplates Christ on the cross.

Does the light burst from inside himself or from the heavens? On his knees, meditating, Francis so empathizes with Jesus that for a moment, Francis becomes like the Savior and, at the same time, sees a vision of the Christ, a six-winged seraph alight with flames. The vision appears all around him. The light of Christ, some say, is so bright and full that some mule drivers in the valley rise from their beds, thinking it is day.[2]

Christ appears to him first so that he might know the blessing of the love of Jesus. Then, afterward, the wounds. The stigmata appear on Francis's hands, his feet, and his side so that he might feel the full pain and anguish of the passion of Christ, just as he begged to know. Suffering and blessing are finally entwined in the body, heart, and mind of one man.

37

To Each Her Own Grief

*W*E *ALL RESPONDED* in our own ways to this grief. I wanted us to get all our feelings out, to express our tears, to admit he was dying. My mom wanted to honor Dad's way of dying. It seemed as though he wasn't ready to say he was through. He wasn't ready to take out the feeding tube, even though it was prolonging his suffering.

While Elena and I hovered around Mom and urged the emotional sharing, Heatherly wanted to be alone, to keep moving on with the tasks of her life.

And Dad? He wouldn't explain how he was feeling. Maybe he mistrusted his emotions because they weren't rational. I wanted nothing but feeling. And I didn't know how to talk to him. Instead, he seemed to turn further inward. If he was taking stock of his life, we didn't know it. If he had regrets, sadness, grief, or dread, he didn't communicate that.

I had to accept that he needed to suffer in his own way, even if that meant he suffered longer.

When it was time for me to return home to Plow Creek, I dreaded the goodbye. Even though no one was willing to say so outright, I knew that unless I could make it back to Texas for the very end, it would probably be the last time I'd see Dad alive.

It seemed that Dad dreaded the goodbye too.

The night before I left, Mom came out from his room and leaned down to whisper to me: "Your dad says you can come in now. But he wants me to stay with him."

At first, I was angry. "He wants you to stay with him? Why? Is he afraid of me and my emotions?"

She shrugged, caught between my emotional needs and those of my father.

"Well, I wasn't planning on saying goodbye tonight anyway," I said. "Can I do it tomorrow?"

"I will go talk to him."

As she left, I began to weep. I was so very, very sad: sad that he was dying and sad that I couldn't tell him how sad it made me. I felt stifled too, like a little child being shushed for being too emotional.

When Mom came back we decided it would be best to do final goodbyes tomorrow.

The next morning, as I prayed my way through packing and getting Annalee ready, I wondered if I should insist on expressing the words and emotions that he didn't have the energy for. Should I blurt out my pain and grief to him? How was I supposed to say goodbye to him for good?

He looked so frail and grey when I stood at the doorway, waiting for him to see me. Even though my mom kept him as clean as she could, the room was cloaked in the smell of his internal decay.

He beckoned me over with his elegant, pale fingers. I didn't know what to say or do, but as soon as I reached the bed, he clasped my hand. Despite his lack of nutrition, his hands were as soft as they'd always been. I'm not sure if I brought his fingers up to my pregnant belly or if he did. But his hand rested there when he began to pray.

It was like the most tender of biblical moments, a dying patriarch blessing his child for the final time. In so many of those deathbed stories in the Old Testament, there is mischief, greed, pain, and ceremony. I think part of me felt bereft of the cultural norms that would urge me and my father to share this moment emotionally, not only with one another but also with our family and community.

There was no scribe but me to record his last words to me. But I was so focused on the fact that this was the final moment, that I might not ever see him again, that I don't remember exactly what he said. I know he blessed the baby in my belly, and he spoke a prayer for our family and our safe travels. I left the tears on my cheeks, not willing to wipe them or break the fragile moment.

When he was finished praying and could see that I was crying, I recognized his vulnerability for that moment. I think he was sad in a way he couldn't express, but he was unable to lean into it. It would have been out of character for me to drape myself across him and weep, and I know he would have hated for me to do so. Still, some ancient call of communal grief nudged me with soft longings.

But instead of wailing over him, I stood there quietly until he said gently, "Well, the morphine makes me tired."

It was my cue to leave. And I took it.

"I love you, Daddy," I said as I got to the door, blowing kisses at him.

He mouthed the same words to me and blew back a weak kiss. And then I left.

* * *

Matthew and I promised each other we would not lose our temper at this meeting.

It was the first community meeting since I'd returned from Texas. We'd gone around and around about it during Christmas, but our final decision had been put off with my extended stay in Texas. Matthew had given his notice that he was quitting his job on the farm.

When suggestions for radical change were met during our community meeting with what I saw as passive caution, I sighed. This wasn't going to happen the way I thought it would. I imagined myself to be on the same page as the most rational of my friends and neighbors. Our criteria for hanging on for this last gasp: Would the community embrace radical change, or would it die? It seemed that most of the community members didn't see that embracing the status quo would lead to a slow death.

Some even suggested that a time of grief was necessary, perhaps even up to a year. While I agreed that we needed to mourn, I didn't think that personal grief should stop the community from moving forward. If a whole year was needed, by the time the grieving period was over, we would be settled back into old habits, and the momentum would be lost.

Matthew lost his temper midway through the meeting, and we realized it was too late for us.

It was time to admit that we were leaving.

* * *

During the hours when she wasn't caring for my father, when his needs still necessitated her presence nearby twenty-four hours a day, my mom went through old pictures of us, many of them a combination of photos from my grandmother's house and the boxes of pictures that lingered for decades in the top of my mom's closet.

She separated them by child, one box for each of us, and began to scan them onto her computer. Off and on, she would email me a picture from my childhood. But one in particular, one of my dad and me when I was nineteen, hit me with grief so hard that I couldn't look at it again for a few days. Probably because it reminded me of the moments I was most present with my dad: when we were traveling together.

In the photo, I am still in college, studying abroad for a semester in Oxford. Dad met me there and took me to Italy. It is the stage of my life when I feel so personally inadequate that I desperately try to be unique. My hair is highlighted and twisted in funky knots. I wear slightly outrageous outfits.

Someone snaps a picture of us on a bridge in Venice. In the photo, I stand slightly behind him, my cheek resting against his shoulder. We are matching in our long black coats, comfortable with silences, both feeling the quiet excitement of seeing new places and eating new foods.

Until I saw this picture, I forgot how much I longed to emulate him then, how in his introspective and often mysterious quietude he understood a deep part of me that no one else did. I know I bought that long black coat that I am wearing in the photo to match the one he started wearing in the early 1990s when he began traveling so often to Russia.

Looking at the photo, I can suddenly recall the soft warmth of his traveling cloak against my cheek. Instead of the lingering stench of his hospice room, full of the odor of bodily fluids, bedsores, and unwashed hair, I smell the musky clean scent of my dad, my real dad. Not the cancer-ridden father who was withering away.

The grief pressed us, my sisters, my mom, and me, down to the depths, and in order to find our way to the lights on the surface, we had to push against the tide of pain and swim upward. And it was so tiring. Instead of revisiting good memories, I'd been holding on to frustration and anger. I hadn't been very nuanced in my grief. It all just felt sad and sorry.

I wanted to glean from grief something besides bitterness, but I knew I couldn't do it on my own. God would have to do it for me.

* * *

I remembered the pain and grief I'd felt when the two families decided to move away from Plow Creek. I understood their reasons, but it was as if they'd decided to break up with us. They'd moved on and left us to pick up the pieces.

I had to keep reminding myself of that feeling when Matthew and I decided to start telling people we would leave after our fourth baby was born in the summer.

Matthew and I were having trouble understanding why some of our neighbors still had hope for the future of Plow Creek, why they wanted to stay and try to piece a life together. Was it a stubborn protest against change? Was it fear of the unknown? Was it that many of them had no other place to go? Or was there a genuine hope for the community, a hope that we were just missing?

I can remember my parents talking about how painful it was when someone left their church for another church in town. From the outside, this seemed petty and childish. It wasn't as if they were leaving the church altogether, or even the denomination. They were just changing buildings.

But in our community, where our lives were so interconnected, from work to home to church, leaving felt more like we were breaking off from our whole family. As Matthew sold off the livestock and hay to pay for the money the farm owed us, it felt a bit like a divorcing couple dividing up their possessions.

"This is why no one comes back to live at Plow Creek once they leave," said Matthew.

He was right. It was too painful. But if it hadn't been painful, we would have stayed.

I had to accept that people were grieving. Sarah and Margaret had both lost their husbands. They needed a grieving period. In the deaths of Rich, David, and Jim, community members had lost friends.

Grief turned some of us inward. For some of us, it highlighted dysfunction. For others of us, it blinded us to the reality of dysfunction.

For Matthew and me, who had always had trouble making decisions when there were copious options, all of these griefs and transitions finally looked like billboards with gaudy neon arrows pointing away from where we were now. They were signs that even we could no longer ignore.

38

Interlude:
At the End

*F*RANCIS NEVER RECOVERS physically from his stigmata wounds. Not that he would want to—not only
does he consider his wounds a gift, a blessing from God
for this poor servant, but these wounds are the physical
manifestation of what Francis has longed for throughout
his relationship with God. He wants to fully experience and
encounter God. For many of his followers, this is a strange
way for God to grace Francis. When a fellow brother seeks
to pray for Francis, asking that his suffering be lessened,
Francis rebukes him and, although weak from his pains,
gets on his knees and thanks God for his suffering. He even
asks that he not be spared more pain.

Francis understands this foolish wisdom: God's love
makes itself fully realized on the cross. Francis knows finally that what overflows from the "divine heart" is what
pours out of his hands, feet, and side on Mount Verna from

the stigmata wounds: the "suffering love that God feels for the world."[1]

In the last year of his life, Francis is more circumspect and troubled. He feels that "God had graced him, Christ had pierced him, and now the devil was hounding him."[2] When he is nearly blind and disfigured from painful treatments and suffering from great pains, not only does he ask to be closer to his beloved Clare but he begins to write his famous "Canticle of the Creatures," a song so different from the biblical and religious language he's been steeped in that it must be a work of art.[3]

What a tragedy for the saint who loves creatures so much, who preaches to the birds and makes a friend of a wolf, to be nearly blind when he dictates the most beautiful song giving praise to God for the earth, its creatures, and its celestial bodies. When Francis speaks of the moon, he knows that it represents the shadows and cycles of life. When he speaks of the wind, he might be speaking of the Holy Spirit, which blows with purpose and mystery. He understands what the psalmist understood: "The heavens declare the glory of God; the skies proclaim the work of his hands. Day after day they pour forth speech; night after night they reveal knowledge" (Psalm 19:1-2). All of creation communes with God.[4]

And then, there is death. Ironically, it is the suffering he endures because of his wounds that finally leads him to repent of berating his own poor body throughout his life. The little poor man who had considered every creature and creation a beautiful gift from God needs to be taught a lesson in his final days: his own body is also a gift from God.

In the days before his death, Francis begins to move away from his sorrow and into songs of praise, into the joy of his youth. He composes the last verse of the canticle. Francis calls his close companions, Leo and Angelo, to sing to him: "Praise to you, O my Lord, for our Sister Death and the death of the body from whom no one may escape."[5]

And then, as all creatures must, he dies. The rich boy turned poor man leaves the earth and his followers bereft and sorrowful. The little poor man who changed the church one stone at a time is finally free to fully love.

39

Death and the Landscape of Grief

M Y DAD DIED at home on a Thursday afternoon, seemingly of his own choice. It wasn't unexpected, of course. But still, when I brought the kids home from school and piano lessons, from a grocery store run and day-care, I was startled by Angela's presence at the door, inviting my kids over to play.

What shocked me most, though, was Matthew's expression: he walked into the house just after I did, pulled me close to him, and whispered in my ear, "Honey, your dad died a few minutes ago."

I wasn't supposed to be shocked. Still, I cried out, "What? What happened?" as if he'd been in a car accident rather than succumbed to the cancer that had been killing him for two years. I sobbed into Matthew's shirt. "I wasn't ready. I didn't think it would be so soon."

That morning, my dad had been awake and alert, but my mom could tell something was wrong: his food hadn't digested and he was having trouble breathing. When the hospice nurse checked his vitals, she took my mom aside and explained the reality.

"Do you want me to tell him?" the nurse asked.

"Yes, he needs to know. Just be as clinical and unemotional as you can," Mom said.

The nurse told my dad that his lungs were filling up and that he probably had two weeks to live.

"Okay," he said softly. The nurse walked to the door to leave. "Grace and peace," he added.

My mom gave him morphine and a pill under the tongue to ease the discomfort and potential panic of his drowning lungs. "How long do you think this will take to work?" he asked her as the medication began to swim through his system.

"Not long."

Mom went to eat lunch in the next room. After a visitor came to the door bringing food, she went back to check on Dad. She could see his breathing had changed and his eyes had rolled back into his head. A few minutes later, she came back, and it took her a moment before she understood.

"I think he's gone," she said to herself, checking his pulse and then calling my brother-in-law to help her confirm.

My dad had a history of pressing his control, opinion, or position onto a situation with dedication and patient persistence. But when the situation or his position was without hope, he released his hold on it, and he didn't look back.

Once he knew there was nothing else to be done, my dad died the way he wanted: alone, without fuss or messy declarations. With the echo of his words "Grace and peace" left behind in our hearts.

* * *

I dragged the kids outside for a walk. They were too young to understand how desperately I needed the warm weather, even if it was a landscape of dormant fields, melting mud, brittle grey plants lining the bridge and sides of the road, a bright red barn against yellowed grass. Lest I get too excited about the lack of snow and cold, Matthew reminded me that this unseasonably pleasant winter in the Midwest was the result of global warming. I guess we both had our ways of grieving.

This was our first day back at Plow Creek after spending a week in Texas for my father's funeral. We all ate too much or too little, depending on our body's responses to stress. We laid flowers on his coffin and wept over him in a graveside service that he might have hated, but one that his daughters and wife, his grandchildren, and his sons-in-law needed. Then we mourned him at a church memorial service that he had planned before his death, writing his own obituary and the opening remarks he asked Matthew to read, ones that unapologetically deflected attention away from himself.

But his three daughters inserted themselves into his plan, a plan that hadn't included our grief. In the midst of his intellectual, cerebral, worshipful funeral, we spoke of him in ways that might have touched him but also likely would have confused him.

In his plans for a truly humble memorial, he hadn't sidestepped our grief to be unkind; I'm sure he knew we'd miss him terribly. Maybe he thought that if he could deflect attention away from himself, we wouldn't be so sad. But what he hadn't guessed—and what might have annoyed him—was that most people who came to honor him wanted *more* of him. Yes, they loved that this service expressed the man they knew, the one who loved his church and carefully planned each part of his service. But they wanted more of his heart, not more of his head.

That's what I always wanted more of too: more of my dad's heart. I've had to forgive him for not being able to express it. Forgiving my parents is much easier as I raise my own children in the world, desperately aware of the things they will have to forgive me for.

Neva, at eight years old, was the most apt to articulate her feelings. She pulled at one of the brittle sticks that lined the road on our walk and gave one to her little sister. The two sisters created walking sticks out of the weeds while Jude ran ahead.

"I love living on a farm," Neva said. "I hope we never have to leave."

Her comment was not out of the blue, of course; we'd just told our kids a few days before that their daddy had quit the farm. With the death of my father, a fourth baby on the way, and a contracted book due in the summer, this decision could have been considered terrible timing and too much transition for all of us to handle gracefully. On the other hand, these griefs and unknowns pushed us to make decisions we'd been putting off for a while. We were finally ready to say we were moving away. But we weren't quite ready to tell our kids.

During the days after we told the kids about Matthew quitting his job, Neva's questions were astute and understandable: "What does that mean?" "Will we still live here?" "I don't want to move."

Pretty quickly, we wondered if we'd told the kids too soon. Was this burden too big for them, when the unknown could stretch ahead for months? I didn't know how to answer Neva, because we didn't know where we would end up.

Is this something you'll have to forgive me for? I wondered as I watched my children enjoy the only home they'd ever known. I wanted to say to Neva: "I had always hoped I wouldn't have to move either, darling. But if you're alive long enough, life and death move you whether you want to or not."

With so much to traverse—sorrow, a move, a birth, and a book—I wondered what would emerge or depart in the coming year. Maybe tomorrow would be brighter, warmer, and revealing. As C. S. Lewis says in *A Grief Observed*, maybe it would hold "a new landscape" that would show some possibilities for unexpected growth.[1] Or maybe the next day would be dark and empty, a tangled mess of brittle weeds.

Our kids loved their lives at Plow Creek, and they were young enough that even when it was cold, dormant, or brittle, it still felt like the normal cycle of life.

As I watched Neva add more dead flowers to her walking stick, I felt like an eight-year-old girl too: afraid in that visceral way that tingled down the spine. In the way of a child, I wondered how I would face a new place, new friends, and another baby. How would I live life without my daddy? How would I be *me* anymore, when there was a dark, empty space where he used to live?

After we'd returned from Texas and I began to come to terms with my dad's death, I started to retreat from community. Between my grief, caring for my family, carrying a baby, and figuring out where to move, I had nothing to give anymore. I tipped my hat to my anxiety, that old fiend, when it began to emerge again: dark feelings, bad dreams, fears, and failings. I knew I would have to face it again and learn to navigate in the wilderness.

But I wasn't the only one retreating from community.

In the weeks after my father's death, everyone began to come to terms with the collapsing of the community. Angela and I talked about our families' futures, hoping that ours would merge with theirs but knowing that the future was so uncertain for all of us.

Mark and Louise announced that they were moving too. Soon meetings were organized with members of other intentional communities, people with experience and vision and a willingness to listen, pray, and help. Their service to our fractured and dying community was a comforting morsel amid such loss. It gave me hope to think that even if our community was dying, there were other lovers of Jesus who cared, who would support and nurture and lead us in reconciliation and grief.

Dave Bell's health began to decline, and he grew distant, leaving church early, not staying for meals afterward. I could tell he was depressed that his new family was breaking apart. The truth was, he'd seen this coming.

A few months before, just after Natalie and Allan decided to move, Dave told Matthew and me that he'd had a vision. In his prayer time, when he expressed sadness about the future of Plow Creek, God told Dave to pray and wait for forty days. Each day, Dave did just that: he would open his Bible randomly the way Saint Francis did sometimes in a practice called bibliomancy, letting it fall open to any Scripture. Then Dave would pray, and God would tell him to just wait.

For forty days, nothing happened. But on the forty-first day, in the middle of his prayer time, Dave had what he called a "waking vision." In this vision, he was standing in the meadow at Plow Creek when a man dressed in a brown robe walked toward an orchard on the edge of the meadow. The man examined the trees in the orchard, and he began to do three things. First, he cut down three trees and laid them gently to the side of the meadow to take home. Next, he dug under a few more trees, scooped them up whole, and set them aside to transplant. Finally, he approached a group of trees that were covered in decay and fungus. Those trees he chopped down to be burned.

It wasn't until after David, Rich, and Jim passed away that Dave began to understand his vision. The first group of trees represented the three men in the community who had died: the robed man gently laid them to rest. The second group of trees, Dave believed, were those who would leave the community and be what Rich always called "scattered members," transplanted elsewhere but creating their own fruit in other places. The third group was, perhaps, the community that once was: it was time for it to be allowed to die and make room for something else to grow.

Maybe in this culling—in the death and crushing of our ideals and the loss of everything that all of us had put our whole hearts into—something beautiful would emerge. Maybe another community could create something new while honoring what Plow Creek had been.

It was our hope. We were all about to map out new territory together. Then again, maybe there would be no map and we would head blindly into the wilderness, praying that this new movement of life would not be the end of everything we knew about ourselves and our place in the world. Maybe an end was necessary, and maybe it would only be for a moment. As C. S. Lewis says, "In grief nothing 'stays put.' One keeps on emerging from a phase, but it always recurs. Round and round. Everything repeats."[2]

Perhaps both my small family unit and my beloved, crumbling church family would eventually emerge from that spiral, from the repetition of old fears, feelings, and sadness, with a new map. And by following charted courses or lands unexplored, we would have something to tell the world and each other—whether perilous, brutal, or exquisite—of the landscape we traversed.

40

Letter to Saint Francis:
To Really Live

Dear Saint Francis,

It is the first week of spring, and I sit in the small cemetery on the Plow Creek property. The daffodils are the earliest signs of life as they begin to bloom around the small gravestones here, some of them marked for infants who died just after birth.

Not for the first time, I wonder, Why is death all around us? What are we going toward? And what will be left behind when we leave Plow Creek?

I know you worried at the end of your life that your ministry would flounder after you died. You didn't feel there was anyone qualified enough to take over. I don't think you felt that way out of arrogance but because you saw the way some of your brothers and your culture could so easily fall away from really following the Jesus you encountered.

I fear the same thing, but not about others. I fear that leaving this place and entering into a different community will make me lazy, that I too will fall away from following Jesus in the way I've begun to learn here. I think I encountered Jesus at Plow Creek among a group of misfits trying to follow Jesus with their whole hearts. I pray that I can live the way of Jesus, even when we leave here, and even when it's hard.

And I have no doubt it will be hard. For we are grieving not only the death of community but also the death of those we love.

Death is so much a part of your story and the story of the Christian mystics. Maybe I should be encouraged in my mystical pursuits by the words of Catholic writer and poet Raïssa Maritain, who once asked, "Can there be a mystical life without death?"[1]

Why is the mystical life bound up with death? Even though death was a painful prospect for you on the mountaintop at La Verna because your ministry was in an unstable place, I think you still embraced death with joy, because it meant that you were so much closer to Christ and his poverty. Didn't you say once, earlier in your life, that "all things should end in poverty, should sing to the world of your pilgrimage and your exile"?[2]

What does it mean for things to end in poverty? The little I've discovered about death, grief, and poverty is that they change you. They strip you bare. And you have to decide what you will do with your utter nakedness, your deep humility and shame.

I know I still struggle with so many things I tried to learn at Plow Creek: simplicity, hospitality, solitude, making my family wider, doing church in a unique way. We longed for a way of community that collapsed while we were there. Sometimes I wonder, What was the point? I know my ideals were crushed long ago. And I think, generally, that's a good thing. My ideals put God and God's kingdom in such a tight box of my own making. I wasn't able to see God's true work in the world until that box was disassembled.

The kingdom of heaven that Jesus preaches in the Gospels often leaves us scratching our heads. How are we to live with one another this way? How are we to give up our possessions, as he commanded the rich young ruler? How are we to live without worry, to visit those in prison, to feed the hungry, to love our enemy?

Maybe the time I spent at Plow Creek gave me a small glimpse into what we are still to strive for despite the seeming impossibility. After all, Francis, you did give away all you had. Your dear Clare fought peacefully against the men who wanted to stop her from worshiping God and began the first order for women. A woman named Dorothy fed and housed the homeless. Simone entered empathetically into the suffering of others, and Margery, despite ridicule, wandered the streets weeping for her love of Jesus.

You longed for Jesus' vision of the kingdom, and you and these women were able to do remarkable things. Maybe the continued longing for the kingdom is the spark of hope that makes God's kingdom come.

But sometimes it's hard to hold on to that longing when everything begins to die. What is the faithful way to grieve death, and how will I keep the important things I've learned here? My world is accustomed to numbing itself from the pain of life and death by keeping itself busy, comfortable, and entertained. But, Francis, you and the other mystics, by your lives, would suggest something else. You were well acquainted with grief, suffering, and the pain of death. And you seemed to hold the nuances confidently, if painfully, even praising God at the end.

The famous mystic-poet Saint John of the Cross endured hardship and persecution so severe that he was eventually left to rot in prison. Saint Francis, I suppose you might have been envious of Saint John's isolation and suffering. But I think you would also see the utterly deep mystical truth: that John found the light of Christ in the dark prison cell.

In his reflection on Saint John's life, Franciscan Don Miller encourages us to take the approach that you, Francis, might take to John's wisdom: "John, in his life and writings, has a crucial word for us today. We tend to be rich, soft, comfortable. We shrink even from words like *self-denial, mortification, purification, asceticism, discipline*. We run from the cross. John's message—like the gospel—is loud and clear: Don't—if you really want to live!"[3]

I do really want to live. Is this kind of living, then, found in death?

As I sit on this cemetery bench, green and mossy from the leftover moisture of snow and air, I am twenty-seven weeks pregnant with our fourth child. I am mourning the death of my dad and the death of community. No, the natural metaphors are not lost on me. After our baby is born, we will move on from this place to another, packing with us all the excitement, grief, worry, and hope we cannot leave behind.

Life, death, suffering, and blessing are huddled so close together that they often resemble one another.

I have learned from my circumstances and from you, Francis, that suffering is part of life. I don't know if there is a reason for it. But I do know that the choice to live into suffering is a mystical contradiction that pushes us deeper into the heart of God's love. For that is where God is and where God's love and presence can be found.

As I write this last letter to you, I want to thank you for teaching me that Jesus is suffering alongside me and alongside so many others, and that to be community we need to suffer with others too. Thank you for your life, for your struggles, for the pain you suffered, and for the lives you've directed toward Jesus.

I believe you and your little garden statue changed me too.

Ever your friend,

Christiana

Epilogue:
Misfits

*O*UR FOURTH BABY was born on a June morning, missing the summer solstice by a handful of labor pains. Although we decided not to find out beforehand, part of me still knew the moment my father prayed a blessing over my belly that our baby would be a boy. When he emerged all red and slippery and I saw his beautiful face, I knew he carried something of his grandfather in him. We gave our son the middle name David, after my father, and the first name Isaac, for the boy whose mother laughed when she discovered she would give birth in her old age. It was only afterward that I remembered our strange visitors Abraham and Sarah, named for Isaac's parents in the Old Testament, and wondered at the convergence of stories, both ancient and new.

In the last weeks of my pregnancy, Plow Creek decided to shut down and hand over the property to another

Mennonite group, one that could bring new life and energy to a place that had, despite its struggles, blessed and encouraged many. When Isaac was two months old, Matthew accepted the call to pastor a Mennonite church in a small town in Ohio. All our neighbors would need to leave eventually. But because my family was the first to go, our leaving precipitated a ceremony of blessing. As I hugged Sarah during our goodbyes, I wept for all that we would be losing, for all that we had lost.

With our living room stacked full of boxes, pictures, and disassembled furniture, the house took on lonely echoes. We had to lean into the physical emptiness of our house even as we dealt with the sorrow of saying goodbye to Dave, Matt and Angela, and their kids. Neva and Jude fell asleep crying for the loss of their best friends. The next morning, with our stuff packed, we left our home, traversing that new landscape in trust and faith.

But the move unsettled us, both literally and spiritually. After all, it had only been six months since my father's death. The dark line down my belly marking my pregnancy hadn't even faded. Yet here we were: new job, new school, new home, and new church. As we entered back into a more "normal" life, I felt the pains of what we'd left behind. With this move away from such a radical way of life, I was scared that I would lose my friend Saint Francis, the mystic and the misfit. I knew that God was with us, but I was scared I would misplace all that I'd learned and gleaned from intentional community and from my dialogue with these great people of faith. I was scared that I would go back to the person I was before community life, before grief, before so many life changes, and before these unlikely saints pointed me toward a more mystical faith.

The church in Ohio showered us with meals, fresh farm produce from their gardens, and offers of childcare. They held our baby so I could eat at potlucks, they taught our children in Sunday school, they invited me to tea, and they sat with us in church. They told us their longings for a more intimate community and wanted us to be a part of that in whatever way we could. We found in this church the rest and solace that we'd been missing for so long.

Still, as Matthew was installed and licensed as pastor, I wondered how I would keep nurturing this mystical faith. As the congregation laid their hands on our family and prayed for us, I envisioned God's Spirit needling its way into our hearts with a tight thread, weaving us together into a multicolored tapestry. I imagined a vision of God blessing our church and our new life. Maybe the imagining of this vision was the closest I would get to an actual revelation of a mystic. But I could still cultivate a mystical faith.

After all, even many of the well-known mystics were circumspect about their visions. I read about Teresa of Ávila, the author of a classic work of mystical contemplation and prayer called *Interior Castle*, who had spectacular, frightening, and ecstatic visions. But she was also a woman who is said to have brought Mary and Martha together: a woman of equal parts action and contemplation.[1] I was heartened to read that Teresa herself didn't place her mystical sight above anyone else's spiritual experience. She noted, "The highest perfection obviously does not consist in interior delights or in great raptures or in vision . . . but in having our will so much in conformity with God's will that there is nothing we know He wills that we do not want with all our desire."[2]

Then I remembered that even Francis was mute about his own mystical experiences. He never spoke of the event of his stigmata; it was only retold by others after his death. Was that because he was less interested in the miracle itself and more interested in how he and his followers should live because of it? Franciscan priest and author Murray Bodo says that "it is part of the genius of St. Francis that he realized the way to God is the way God came to us, not by ascending to some spiritual stratosphere, but by descending and entering our world."[3]

Descending and entering our world. Yes, as I recalled my dialogues with the mystics and what I'd learned from them, I realized something that was obvious if I had only looked. Mystics from other religions have much in common with the Christian mystics: they all long for unity with whatever they call God, for a union with the divine. But what distinguishes Christian mystics is the incarnation of Christ. Christian mystics long to be in union with the God who made himself small, who came to suffer alongside his creation, who descended and entered into our world, and who called us to join him in that truly baffling kind of love.

The mystics tapped into this love. Theirs was the kind of love that propelled them to the fringes of their societies and their churches. The kind of love that made them misfits.

Maybe I will never have the unsettling and euphoric visions of the mystics. But I have found the stirrings of a mystical faith in striving for simplicity, in the ways of contemplation, in showing hospitality, in living in community and entering into the suffering of others, and in facing the darkest and most painful parts of being human: sin, suffering, and death.

The very pillars of faith—whether they be the mystics, the saints, or the men and women of the Bible—were unsure, broken, wandering, and lost. They failed and they triumphed, but they were always longing. Maybe the key to nurturing a mystical faith is in the longing itself. Even though I sometimes feel tormented by my own failings, by anxious thoughts and worries, I can keep the mystics with me by loving with a misfit kind of love. By holding on to the God that the mystics and misfits held on to. By always longing for union with the God who descended into our world in weakness and is madly, madly in love with us, no matter how much we fail.

Acknowledgments

THANK YOU to all the lovely folks at Herald Press for making the publication of my first book feel so magical. Perhaps my next book will be a medieval Irish mystery novel just to match the incredible cover! Thank you to Valerie Weaver-Zercher for being a kind, gifted, encouraging, and present editor; for "getting" my work, appreciating the quirks, lamenting the challenges, and understanding when life was becoming too overwhelming to write. Amy Gingerich, thank you for taking a chance on my proposal at the Festival of Faith and Writing and for last-minute video chats to talk about tricky chapters.

I relied most heavily on these authors both in the writing of this book and in my spiritual walk, and I am so grateful for their body of work: Jon Sweeney, Richard Rohr, Ilia Delio, Dorothy Day, and Henri Nouwen. Even though I don't quote or cite her, you can always assume that Madeleine L'Engle (otherwise known in my writer's group as Saint Madeleine) inspires me in everything I read and write. Thank you to Greg Wolfe and editors Cathy Warner and Jan Vallone for taking me on as a writer for *Good Letters*, the place where I first started writing about the mystics. Thank you to inspiring writers like Jessica Mesman Griffith and Kaya Oakes who write about Catholicism, and to all my lovely workshop-mates at the Glen 2016: your words about my first letter to Saint Francis gave me the confidence to keep writing the rest of this book. Thank you to Julia Walsh and Joan Weisenbeck, Franciscan Sisters of Perpetual Adoration, for helping me write as accurately as possible about your spiritual father, Saint Francis. And thank you to Linda Hicks for bringing me back *The Little Flowers of Saint Francis* from Assisi.

Thank you to Seth Haines for your generous help with my contract. For your lyrical writing and endorsements, thank you to Amber C. Haines and Christie Purifoy.

Thanks to Ron and the other Princeton Public Library folks for the coffee and for allowing me to spend hours writing in your study rooms and letting my kids hang out in the children's area on rainy days. To Lisa, Sharon, and the other wonderful librarians at Tiskilwa Public Library, thank you for ordering obscure books about the mystics and then calling me when they were overdue and renewing them for me over the phone. Local libraries are havens for both misfits and desperate mothers.

To Kendra and Ryan Juskus, thank you for conversations about writing and parenthood, for sending me scholarly articles about mystics, and for making me a godmother. I am also grateful to the writers, artists, and friends who have supported and inspired me over the years: Katie Munnik, Christopher Lapinel, Heather Munn, Matt "Redbeard" Adams, and Catherine Tripp. And thank you to Tim Otto for your life-giving book *Oriented to Faith*.

To Jen Kilps, my companion to Genevieve's castle and across the landscape of grad school in Scotland, thank you for giving me my first idealistic notions about intentional community.

Thank you to my Brentwood church and school family for nurturing my childhood faith, caring so much about my life and writing, and offering rigorous biblical training that still stays with me today. Thank you to my teachers Deb Holloway and Linda Pimentel for helping me develop an early love of reading and writing.

I am so thankful for Ann, Amy, Kimberly, Heather, Holly, and Tracy, who have taught me how to laugh at myself. I hope you never listen to Enya without thinking of me.

Angela Adams, you are more than just a neighbor, and our kids are more than just best friends. Thank you for becoming my sister and loving me even at my worst. And thank you for your marvelous edits. I am grateful to my friends Natalie, Dan and Camille, Gina and Dan, Sheena, and Jessica Boggs, who entertained my kids, made us meals, bought baby clothes, and simply kept me sane with your love and understanding.

Jessica Goudeau, thank you for your constant and deep friendship and kinship, for reading my writing for nearly twenty years and telling me to keep going. You've been an encouragement in too many ways to count, and our friendship has led to both my husband (thanks to Jocelyn for that, too) and my writing career. What other best friend can top that? To you, Jessica, and the rest of my writing accomplices, Stina Kielsmeier-Cook, Amy Peterson, Kelly Nikondeha, and D. L. Mayfield: Your voices have been the soundtrack to many of the mundane, beautiful, and painful parts of my life. Thank you for inspiring me with your writing, your activism, and your lived faith; for listening to me talk about jam-making, chickens, community life, and young adult novels; and for being my agents, editors, writing partners, and friends. Let's face it, I really wrote this book because I wanted to be cool like you.

Thank you to David Janzen and Sally Schreiner Youngquist for your wisdom and mentorship in the last few years, even amid the painfulness of the loss of Plow Creek. To those of you who trusted me to use your names and memories: Margaret, Sarah, Mark, Louise, Dave, Matt and Angela, Natalie and Allan, and the rest of my Plow Creek family. These years were hard, and these years were lovely. You taught me so much about radical Christianity, about living fully for Jesus. I will miss you. But I know, as Rich knew, that our dispersing doesn't leave us without a membership in the body of Christ. We will be scattered members together.

To Craig and Debbie, I couldn't have written this without your love, support, and encouragement. Thank you for always coming when we called, for loving our kids, for cleaning our house, for cooking meals galore, and for praying constantly. You are the best second parents a daughter-in-law could ask for.

Thank you to my McDaniel, Coggin, Sullivan, and Peterson nieces, nephews, and brothers- and sisters-in-law: you are a joy to be with, every single one of you. A special shout-out to Addie: I'm thanking you because I said I would, and I hope you write a book (or an album) one day too.

Heatherly and Elena, thank you for always showing me unconditional love and support. This book is for you, for the times when your brave voices were shushed and you felt discouraged from following your intuitions and vocations. You are both fierce warriors, and I'm humbled by your perseverance in the midst of profound challenges. I'm proud to call you my sisters and best friends. Worley sisters unite!

Mom, thank you for the Psalms, the tearful evening chats, the long-distance theological discussions, and the hilarious moments when we laughed over the absurdities of grief. Thank you for being my first reader for so many years, and for being my confidante. I cannot write of your strength, your wisdom, or your ferocious love without weeping, so I will just leave you with a quote, attributed to Jodi Picoult, that perfectly encapsulates you: "My mother . . . she is beautiful, softened at the edges and tempered with a spine of steel. I want to grow old and be like her" (From the novel *Handle with Care*, 2009).

To my lovelies, my babies Neva, Jude, Annalee, and Isaac: You are all brave, unique, and beloved. I hope you read these words one day and understand our lives at Plow Creek a little better. Until then, enjoy the innocence of knowing very little of the challenges your parents faced and matured from in these years. I love you to God and back.

And to my dearest, Matthew: Thank you for being my companion in life, for learning and growing with me, for standing beside me through ten years of adventure, loss, and joyful surprises. You are my friend, my love, and my rock. I know the next ten could bring us both gifts and sorrows, but I would gladly walk beside you there and anywhere. You are truly my *Matthaios*, a "gift of YAHWEH."

And finally, to other aspiring mystics and budding misfits: may we listen with keen ears and open hearts to the voices that challenge, disturb, and offer strange hope to us from the fringes.

Notes

Prologue: Mystics

1 This and the preceding quotation are from McGinn, *The Essential Writings*, xiv.

2 The term *mysticism* is from the seventeenth century but was used more in the nineteenth century.

3 McGinn, *The Essential Writings*, xiv.

4 While some more modern mystics in the Christian tradition, like the French philosopher Simone Weil, placed themselves outside the church because of conviction, there is still a sense of dialogue *with* the church and also a view to reform what has, at times, become a stagnant religion.

5 Sweeney, *The Enthusiast*, 207. Sweeney quotes Joanne Schatzlein and Daniel Sulmasy from their 1987 *Franciscan Studies* article, "The Diagnosis of St. Francis: Evidence for Leprosy."

6 Randy Harris, "The Sermon on the Mount: A Contemporary Interpretation," sermon, Highland Church of Christ, Abilene, TX, January 8, 2017.

7 Randy Harris, email message to author, March 22, 2016.

2. Interlude: The Simple Saint

1 This and the preceding quotation are from Dennis et al., *St. Francis and the Foolishness of God*, 105–6.

2 Ugolino, *The Little Flowers*, 62.

3 Sweeney, *When Saint Francis Saved*, 109.

4 Thomas of Celano, *The Lives of St. Francis of Assisi*, 148.

3. First Impressions

1 Global Anabaptist Mennonite Encyclopedia Online, s.v. "Simplicity (1958)," by Harold S. Bender, Nanne van der Zijpp, and Cornelius Krahn, accessed October 3, 2016, http://gameo .org/index.php?title=Simplicity_(1958). Mennonites are an off-shoot of the Anabaptist movement that emerged during the Reformation (the term *Anabaptist* was originally derogatory, I might add). Anabaptists, and later Mennonites, were often killed for their belief that adults, not infants, should be baptized.

2 Quoted in Sweeney, *The Enthusiast*, 86.

3 Sweeney, *Francis of Assisi in His Own Words*, 52.

5. Interlude: The Spoiled Charmer

1 Sweeney, *The Enthusiast*, 65.

2 Ibid., 27.

3 Ibid., 43.

8. Decay

1 At the time of this book's publication, very little other information on Conrad Wetzel was available. Sources of information about Wetzel's abuse mentioned in this chapter include "IMC/CDC Statement about Conrad Wetzel's Confession," May 1992, private collection; "Plow Creek Fellowship's Response to Conrad Wetzel's Confession," May 9, 1992, private collection; "A Letter to All Active Ordained and Licensed Leaders in the Illinois Mennonite Conference," May 8, 1992, private collection.

9. Interlude: Saint Francis and His Lady

1 Green, *God's Fool*, 69.

2 Dennis et al., *St. Francis and the Foolishness of God*, 13.

3 Sweeney, *The Enthusiast*, 53.

4 Bodo, *The Threefold Way of Saint Francis*, 13.

5 Ibid., 10.

6 Sources for the information in this section include Green, *God's Fool*; Sweeney, *The Enthusiast*.

7 Green, *God's Fool*, 79.

8 A hair shirt is a garment made from rough animal skin or hair that is worn under clothes, close to the skin, thus acting as an irritant, or act of penance.

9 Sweeney, *The Enthusiast*, 60. Francis says this before a public meeting that his father and the bishop of Assisi have summoned him to.

10. Letter to Saint Francis: The Lunacy of Love

1 Richard Rohr, "Where You Can't Be Bought Off," Daily Meditations, Center for Action and Contemplation, October 7, 2016, https://cac.org/cant-bought-off-2016-10-07/. The text is adapted from Richard Rohr, *Eager to Love: The Alternative Way of Francis of Assisi* (Cincinnati: Franciscan Media, 2014), 36–40.

2 Green, *God's Fool*, 82.

3 Ibid.

4 Ibid., 99.

12. Interlude: The Do-Gooder

1 This and the preceding quotation are from Coles, *Dorothy Day*, 4.

2 Day, *The Long Loneliness*, 149.

3 Ibid.

4 Day, *Loaves and Fishes*, 27.

5 Ibid., 10.

6 Ibid.

7 Ibid.

14. Interlude: Commune Farms

1 Day, *Loaves and Fishes*, 44.

2 Ibid., 46–47.

3 Ibid., 49.

4 Ibid., 58.

5 Ibid., 60.

16. Letter to Dorothy Day: A Saint for Difficult People

1 The title of this letter is taken from James Parker, "A Saint for Difficult People," *The Atlantic*, March 2017, https://www.theatlantic.com/magazine/archive/2017/03/a-saint-for-difficult-people/513821/.

2 Robert Ellsberg, introduction to *Dorothy Day, Selected Writings: By Little and By Little*, xviii.

3 Parker, "A Saint for Difficult People."
4 Nouwen, *Reaching Out*, 71.

17. Winter
1 Merton, *Contemplative Prayer*, 27.
2 Ibid., 25.

18. Interlude: Margery Kempe
1 Kempe, *The Book of Margery Kempe*, 10–11.
2 Ibid., 42–43.

19. Mother God
1 King, *Christian Mystics*, 137.

20. Interlude: Clare of Assisi
1 Sweeney, *The Enthusiast*, 119.

22. Interlude: The Cloister of the World
1 *Clare of Assisi: Early Documents*, 2nd ed., ed. and trans. Regis J. Armstrong, (New York: The Franciscan Institute, 1993), 67, quoted in Sweeny, *The Enthusiast*, 122.
2 Merton, *Contemplative Prayer*, 29.
3 Delio, *Franciscan Prayer*, 127.
4 Ibid., 9.
5 Ibid.

24. Letter to Clare of Assisi: Mother of God
1 Delio, *Clare of Assisi*, 4.
2 Ibid., 2.
3 Claiborne, Wilson-Hartgrove, and Okoro, "January 11," in *Common Prayer*, 101.
4 Ibid.

25. A New Kind of Family
1 Otto, *Oriented to Faith*, 13.
2 Ibid.
3 Ibid., 14.

26. Interlude: What Does the Lord Require?
1 This scene, originally from Ugolino, *The Little Flowers*, is retold in Sweeney, *The Enthusiast*, 126–28.
2 Sweeney, *The Enthusiast*, 128.
3 Ibid.

28. Interlude: Awkward Anarchist
1 Weil, *Waiting for God*, xvi–xvii.
2 Ibid., xv.
3 Ibid., xvi.
4 Ibid., 3–4.

30. Interlude: Awakening
1 Terry Tastard, "Simone Weil's Last Journey," *America*, April 9, 2001, http://www.americamagazine.org/issue/335/article/simone-weils-last-journey.
2 Weil, *Waiting for God*, xxii.
3 Ibid., xxvi.

31. Letter to Simone Weil: The Miracle of Attention
1 Weil, *Waiting for God*, 62.
2 Ibid., 64.
3 Ibid.

33. Interlude: Between the Angel and the Lady
1 Ugolino, *The Little Flowers*, 185.

34. Our Sacred Cows
1 Delio, *Clare of Assisi*, ix.

35. Hospice
1 Merton, *Contemplative Prayer*, 27.

36. Interlude: A Broken Body
1 Ugolino, *The Little Flowers*, 194.
2 Ibid., 195.

38. Interlude: At the End

1 Dennis et al., *St. Francis and the Foolishness of God*, 128.

2 Sweeney, *The Enthusiast*, 196–97.

3 Ibid., 196.

4 Saint Francis's thoughts on the elements are taken from Dennis et al., *St. Francis and the Foolishness of God*, 104–20, 162–65.

5 Sweeney, *Francis of Assisi in His Own Words*, 91.

39. Death and the Landscape of Grief

1 C. S. Lewis, *A Grief Observed*, 71.

2 Ibid., 69.

40. Letter to Saint Francis: To Really Live

1 Sweeney, *When Saint Francis Saved the Church*, 128.

2 Sweeney, *The Enthusiast*, 205.

3 Don Miller, OFM, "Saint John of the Cross: Saint of the Day for December 14," Franciscan Media, accessed October 9, 2017, https://www.franciscanmedia.org.

Epilogue: Misfits

1 King, *Christian Mystics*, 150.

2 Ibid., 153.

3 Bodo, *The Threefold Way of Saint Francis*, 22.

Bibliography

Almedingen, E. M. *St. Francis of Assisi: A Great Life in Brief.* New York: Alfred A. Knopf, 1971.

Bodo, Murray, OFM. *The Threefold Way of Saint Francis.* New York: Paulist Press, 2000.

Boff, Leonardo. *Francis of Rome and Francis of Assisi.* Maryknoll, NY: Orbis Books, 2014.

Claiborne, Shane, Jonathan Wilson-Hartgrove, and Enuma Okoro. *Common Prayer: A Liturgy for Ordinary Radicals.* Grand Rapids: Zondervan, 2010.

Coles, Robert. *Dorothy Day: A Radical Devotion.* Boston: De Capo Press, 1987.

Day, Dorothy. *Loaves and Fishes.* Maryknoll, NY: Orbis Books, 1997.

———. *The Long Loneliness.* San Francisco: Harper, 1981.

Delio, Illia. *Franciscan Prayer.* Cincinnati: St. Anthony Messenger Press, 2004.

———. *Clare of Assisi: A Heart Full of Love.* Cincinnati: Franciscan Media, 2007.

Dennis, Marie, Joseph Nangle, Cynthia Moe-Lobeda, and Stuart Taylor. *St. Francis and the Foolishness of God*. Maryknoll, NY: Orbis Books, 1993.

Ellsberg, Robert. Introduction to *Dorothy Day, Selected Writings: By Little and By Little*, xv–xli. Edited by Robert Ellsberg. Maryknoll, NY: Orbis Books, 1992.

Emling, Shelley. *Setting the World on Fire: The Brief, Astonishing Life of St. Catherine of Siena*. New York: St. Martin's Press, 2016.

Green, Julien. *God's Fool: The Life and Times of Francis of Assisi*. San Francisco: Harper and Row, 1985.

Julian of Norwich. *Revelations of Divine Love*. Translated by Elizabeth Spearking. London: Penguin, 1998.

Keating, Thomas. *Open Mind, Open Heart: 20th Anniversary Edition*. New York: Bloomsbury, 2006.

Kempe, Margery. *The Book of Margery Kempe*. Translated by B. A. Windeatt. London: Penguin Books, 1994.

King, Ursula. *Christian Mystics: Their Lives and Legacies throughout the Ages*. New Jersey: Hidden Spring, 1998.

Lewis, C. S. *A Grief Observed*. San Francisco: Harper, 1989.

MacDonald, Elizabeth. *Skirting Heresy: The Life and Times of Margery Kempe*. Cincinnati: Franciscan Media, 2014.

McBrien, Richard P. *Lives of the Saints: From Mary and St. Francis of Assisi to John XXIII and Mother Theresa*. San Francisco: Harper, 2001.

McGinn, Bernard, ed. *The Essential Writings of Christian Mysticism*. New York: The Modern Library, 2006.

Merton, Thomas. *Contemplative Prayer*. New York: Image, 1996.

Nouwen, Henri. *Reaching Out*. New York: Image, 1986.

Otto, Tim. *Oriented to Faith: Transforming the Conflict Over Gay Relationships*. Eugene, OR: Cascade Books, 2014.

Rohr, Richard. *Eager to Love: The Alternative Way of Francis*. Cincinnati: Franciscan Media, 2014.

———. *Everything Belongs: The Gift of Contemplative Prayer*. New York: Crossroad, 2003.

———. *The Naked Now: Learning to See as the Mystics See*. New York: Crossroad, 2009.

Smith, James. *You Are What You Love*. Grand Rapids, MI: Brazos Press, 2016.

Sweeney, Jon. *The Enthusiast: How the Best Friend of Francis of Assisi Almost Destroyed What He Started*. Notre Dame, IN: Ave Maria Press, 2016.

————, trans. *Francis of Assisi in His Own Words: The Essential Writings*. Brewster, MA: Paraclete Press, 2013.

————. *When Saint Francis Saved the Church*. Notre Dame, IN: Ave Maria Press, 2014.

Talbot, John Michael. *The Lessons of St. Francis*. New York: Dutton, 1997.

Teresa of Ávila. *Interior Castle*. Translated and edited by E. Allison Peers. New York: Dover, 2007.

Thomas of Celano. *The Lives of St. Francis of Assisi*. Translated by A. G. Ferrers Howell. London: Methuen, 1908.

Thurman, Howard. *Jesus and the Disinherited*. Boston: Beacon Press, 1996. First published 1949 by Abingdon-Cokesbury.

Ugolino. *The Little Flowers of Saint Francis*. Translated by W. Heywood. Assisi: Edizioni Porziuncola, n.d.

Weil, Simone. *Waiting for God*. Translated by Emma Craufurd. New York: Harper Perennial, 2009.

The Author

CHRISTIANA N. PETERSON is a regular contributor to *Good Letters*, an *Image Journal* blog, and she has published pieces on death, fairy tales, and farm life at Christianity Today Women, Off the Page, and *Art House America*. Peterson lives with her husband and their four children in Ohio. Find more of her writing and connect with her at Christiananpeterson.com.